"At times such as now, when you sit down
and start remembering the things you have done and seen,
and especially the things you have felt,
then you know you want to keep going on."

- Ernie Pyle

bowling
for.
christmas
& other tales from the road

Mark Dvorak

BOOKBABY.COM

CONTENTS

Airport Day

I'm on my way to Portland this morning. My banjo and duffle are checked, my guitar and backpack are with me. It seems like there are a million other people here at the airport in Chicago, and we are all waiting and hurrying and eating, keeping ourselves occupied, keeping ourselves together, enduring the unsettledness of air travel. I don't fly often enough to have become real good at it. I bring too much stuff, and I leave too much time. And I am still suspicious of any vehicle that goes faster than, or flies higher off the ground than my little truck. I am further suspicious of any mode of transportation which does not require me to be the driver.

One of these million is a young man who appears to be new to airports. He has longish brown hair and thick sideburns. His chin is bearded and it looks as if he is traveling alone. He wanders slowly down the long hall of gates at the American Airlines terminal, alternately checking his boarding pass and the sequence of gate numbers posted overhead.

A group of three women sashay past in the other direction. Thirty-fiveish, bubbling and chatty, they look happy to be traveling together. All are dressed colorfully this summer afternoon, skirts flowing, high heels clacking. A man pushing a heaping luggage cart lags behind. It appears they have also brought too much stuff with them.

To my left, a mom smiles between sips of juice. Her two boys are squeezed together in the seat next to hers, their young faces bright with anticipation. A few aisles across from them, an African-American gentleman chews his sandwich. He is sporting a ball cap and wears a knit shirt. A single shoulder bag rests at his feet. He chews slowly, scanning the passing river of humanity. He is the very picture of cool collectedness in this buzzing hive of voices, ringtones and public address announcements. Everywhere around him people fidget and stretch. They dial and type and yawn. Glassy eyes gaze toward something far off. We are all pilgrims awaiting departure, readying ourselves on another airport day, for the next new thing.

At this point in my life, I have seen a million other guitar players, and it dawns on me today that good ones are a lot like good air travelers. Mostly, they are self-reliant types, alert and always learning as they go. They are problem solvers who are able to focus and juggle. They borrow ideas from others as needed, and they come to regard firsthand experience as the hardened truth against which all else is to be tested. Good guitar players tend to be reserved and helpful to those with less experience. They learn how to help and when to help, and when not to. And generally speaking, good guitar players care little about what anyone else may think, so long as they get to do their work; so long as they get to where they are going.

And by watching the veterans - the good guitar players who have been at it a long time - we learn to stay cool and to chew slowly. They model awareness and have learned to get along comfortably without all the gadgets and paraphernalia. They teach us to pay attention to the little things so we can better improvise and plan. They teach us to leave the excess baggage behind and to travel light. It really is the only way to fly.

One Man's Hands

It is raining again, and the Cubs game has been delayed. It is quiet in the house, and I am enjoying the sound of the rain, remembering things from the recent summer past. In many ways it has been a good summer. There has been plenty of work, and I've crossed paths with many good people. Summer has meant road trips and outdoor concerts. It has meant shorts and bare feet and barbecue on the new Weber. Summer has meant practicing on the back porch with fresh coffee, watching the big maple tree move in the breeze.

And as with a lot of boys, this summer and all the other ones before it have meant playing ball. This was my last summer of ball playing, though, and this time I really mean it. Even as my team contends for the league title, my season is finished; my ball playing days now concluded for all time. The decision came easily enough this week due to not one, but two incidents, involving poor judgement and a specific finger on my left hand.

The first incident happened in June, the season still young and hope still eternal. An attempt to catch a sinking line drive left me trying to shake off a swollen ring finger. In Chicago, nurse Mary thought it was broken and said, "Go see a doctor." When I later showed it to farmer Hugh of Bartonville, Illinois, he simply nodded and said, "yep," the way a farmer might, without making the sound of the 'p.' Let the record show that I finished the game with two hits and five runs batted in.

The latest incident occurred about a week ago and was messier and sorrier than the one before. My finger was splinted and wrapped and for a time had come to resemble an armless little mummy with a nosebleed. So this time I am hanging them up for good. Autumn will bring healing and recovery, and the cleats and bats and balls will go up to the attic, along with the screens and the porch furniture. Come opening day next spring, I promise to not give them another look.

So the last few days I've mostly been laying around, watching it rain, taking Advil and waiting for summer to wind down. I've had plenty of time to think about playing ball and growing older. I've had time to think about my hands.

When my hands were tough and calloused, I was young and working a night job for a grocery company. I was on a shift with other boys from eleven at night until seven thirty in the morning. When I'd get home from work, I worked at learning guitar and later, five-string banjo. As my hands became more sure on the strings, they also became chafed and coarse from nights unloading trucks, slinging stock and pushing around two hundred pound bales of cardboard.

At some point I started to land performing jobs on the local coffeehouse scene, though I still had to keep my night job. I'd tote my guitar and my five-string banjo off to some little place, and played them as best I could with hands that had turned to dry, cracked shoe leather. I remember meeting lots of musicians around that time. Many were like me, learning, scrambling, trying to improve. Some were more advanced, and others still were already recording and working at music full time. And I remember the occasion of shaking hands with one of these fellows, a full-time polished professional. For the first time I noticed what a musician's hands felt like. And for the first time I felt a kind of uneasiness that my own hands were those of a working stiff.

Soon enough though, I was able to let go of my career as a grunt in the grocery business. Soon enough I found myself scratching out a living, playing music and teaching. Soon enough the recording projects came along, and the tours, and soon enough my hands began to change. After years of coaxing sound from a guitar and a five-string banjo, my fingers turned lean and muscular, the skin on my palms grew smooth and soft.

And I recall the time earlier this summer, coming down off the stage after performing at a music festival in Tennessee. A man wearing overalls waved and walked over. He was a tobacco farmer as it turned out. His name was Jim, and I remember him as a very fine man. Jim had a wide-brimmed straw hat on his head, and his jaw swelled with a plug of tobacco. He said he'd been farming in these parts for more than forty years. He smiled, almost toothless, and said how he liked to come down to hear the old songs each year at the festival. Jim thanked me for making the trip all the way from Chicago. He said some nice things about my playing, and I said some nice things about the people and the country in western Tennessee. It felt good having passed muster with an earthy old-timer like Jim. He'd been listening to music down here for a lot of years.

And then Jim began to talk about his brother and his father, and his mother who passed away when he was young. He began to talk about tobacco farming. Although he loved music and loved to be around it, Jim said that neither he, nor his brother, ever had the time to take up an instrument. There was always too much work to do.

We talked awhile longer and I thanked Jim for our visit. I held out my hand and he grasped it. His grip was steady, his palm was rough and calloused and felt like dry, cracked shoe leather. I felt a kind of uneasiness that my own hands were soft and those of a musician. "So long," said Jim, and he turned. I watched him disappear into the crowd.

Of Songbirds, Salesmen & a Bigger Soul

Today I disassembled my banjo and put a new drumhead on it. Such operations are never simple or clean. There is always a certain amount of jerry-rigging and adjusting and guessing and tinkering. I am reminded of the time I went to the shoe store and asked the salesman for a pair of shoes that felt something like the worn in, beat up loafers that had taken me eight years to break in, to form to my feet and fit to my gait. Of course he had no such shoes in stock, but the new ones he showed me looked like the old ones used to look before I cared about them.

A new banjo head is stiff and makes your banjo sound different. And I cleaned all the dust and corrosion off of some of the innards and tightened everything down to specs. I made a crude modification to the design of the tailpiece, and after a morning and an afternoon of monkeying around with it, and playing it and taking it apart again, then tuning it again then adjusting the neck angle again, it still isn't anything like my old comfortable banjo, the one I took apart this morning after I happened to hear the news that the great tenor Luciano Pavarotti had passed away.

I've never been to the opera, although I've listened to some on the radio. I have been around long enough I think, to most times recognize artistry where and when it occurs, whether I understand it completely or not. I grow evermore thankful for those moments, and could not help but think about Pavarotti while dismantling my beloved Vega banjo. I couldn't help but think that the world has lost another precious songbird. To be sure, I haven't followed his career very closely. A good friend of mine was once a member of the Chicago Lyric Opera, and I remember him all aglow when the great Pavarotti was scheduled to come to Chicago. And I remember him then bemoaning the series of cancellations that ensued, so many that it led the Lyric to no longer require Pavarotti's services. Ever. I think perhaps that's when I began to take some notice of him. If I remember correctly, he said something like, "qualunque," which means, "Whatever."

I remember seeing Pavarotti sing on television with The Three Tenors and being absolutely knocked out by the sounds he was able to make. If you think you don't like opera, or that kind of singing, try making some of those same sounds on your own. Go on into the shower, right now, and turn on the water and begin. After you towel off, you still may not like opera, but you surely will have greater admiration for one who could sing with such power and grace, and at the same time make it look effortless. Pavarotti made singing look like fun. Go ahead, put your pants back on.

I saw Pavarotti sing with the Spice Girls too, on television. When he received harsh criticism for degrading his art by appearing with them, he shrugged it off and said, "Hs reso felici le persone," which means something like, "Nobody cares what you think."

And then at some point Pavarotti left his wife of thirty-seven years and married a woman very much younger than he. The split was messy, the new relationship public. His character was called into question time and again, and time and again he responded, "Sono felice," which means, "Mind your own damned business."

While driving to the hardware store to buy some hardware with which I had hoped to jerry-rig the tailpiece of my Vega, I heard Rudy Giuliani being interviewed on the radio. Rudy is not an opera singer, nor is he Italian. He is Italian-American and campaigning to become the President of the United States. And he talked like a pitchman behind on his sales quota. Not so fast Rudy, I'm not so sure I am interested.

'Il presidente?'

'Prego dio!'

The journalist interviewing him was neither Italian nor Italian-American, but he generally agreed with everything Rudy said and offered a lot of like opinions. Isn't a journalist supposed to ask questions?

"Il vostro parere non importa" roughly means, "Your opinion is not so important." You can look up "Due asini bacio" for yourself.

Seriously Rudy, if you want my vote in the election a year and two months from now, try reading the United States Constitution again, the "Libro di Regola," and talk to me about that on the radio. Everything both you and I need to know is in there, and it strikes me that it may have been awhile since you last looked at it. But what do I know? I am a banjo player on my way to the hardware. Mama mia!

Here's another opinion. The guy who works evenings at the hardware store in town is a saint.

"Questo uomo è un San."

He is a young man and doesn't say much, but he knows where everything is in the store. I showed him the tailpiece to my Vega and showed him the little holes where the pin used to hold it together. Immediately he said, "Let's go back and start digging around." Right away this kid recognized his chance to participate in the holy practice of jerry-rigging, without ever once thinking he had to know the first thing about a banjo.

"Come un Dio."

And when I got back to the car, Rudy and the interviewer were still prattling on, talking about things that anyone with access to a computer and Google.com would be able to call into question. I didn't hear Rudy talk about policy, nor did I hear him offer any meaningful proposals. He may have done so during the seven minutes or so I was in the hardware store, but I went in during a commercial break and I don't think so. Rudy reported very few facts, maybe none, and he generally spoke poorly of others in his own chosen field, those also campaigning to become President.

"Molto a differenza di un Dio."

Then once more the commercials came. A car salesman, a pitch for a vacation package, a medicine commercial, a couple of program teasers, a restaurant ad. I changed the channel, and there was Pavarotti. He was singing "Ave Maria," and it made me cry.

I once had the chance to listen to Kurt Vonnegut, Jr. speak, and I have remembered something that he said. Toward the end of his talk he said, "We are here on earth to fart around. Don't let anyone tell you different."

And Kurt also said, "Art isn't a trade, it's a way to make your soul grow. We become by practicing art, no matter how well or how badly. Practicing art is a way to make your soul bigger."

Luciano, avete un'anima grande. Grazie. Resto nella pace.

The Last Time I Saw John Hartford

The story begins in Philadelphia, and it's the summer before John passed away. There's this huge folk festival, called the Philadelphia Folk Festival, where tens of thousands of people come every summer to this big field, this big grove, and they camp out and they listen to concerts and they jam. There are people everywhere at the Philadelphia Folk Festival. It is the largest folk music festival, I think, in the lower forty-eight states.

We were invited there to do something or other a couple summers ago, and our group went. We had a brief appearance on the main stage as a group, and these other appearances as individuals on smaller stages scattered around the festival grounds.

There was a considerable amount of down time involved between our appearances at Philadelphia that summer. The festival grounds are something like thirty miles away from the hotel, and if you want to go back to the hotel you have to go to a certain place and wait in line for a shuttle bus to return. It's a very involved process, so generally speaking, when you get to the festival site in the morning, you stay there for the entire day.

It was Saturday, as I remember, and all of my other appearances for the day were completed. I did a lot of walking around the grounds in the hours between my last appearance that afternoon and before the main stage concert was to begin that evening. I did a lot of snooping and listening and watching people enjoy themselves. Utah Phillips was originally scheduled to perform on the main stage that evening, but he was sick and couldn't make it. The word was his doctor wouldn't let him fly in from California where he lives, so they called John Hartford. And John said he would come.

I have seen John Hartford play on maybe a couple dozen

occasions. Maybe more. And I've listened to his records, some of them till they wore out. I realize now there are players you listen to so much, like John Hartford, that after a time it's as if you keep them inside of you. And when you see them again in person, it seems almost as if they hopped out of you to come before your eyes and ears before they go back in.

It was late afternoon at the Philadelphia Folk Festival on that Saturday, the summer before John Hartford died. The sun was getting low in the sky and it was warm. I was walking in the field just outside the fence surrounding the last row of the main stage area. And that's when I saw him. I saw him across the field and over the rise, way over on the other side of the vendor booths. He was walking from the place where the shuttle bus drops people off from the hotel, and he was walking with his fiddle. And he was bent over and he looked old. He was far away, but I knew it was him, and I watched him walk all by himself, carrying his fiddle case. He had white shoes on, and it turned out that he wasn't wearing any socks, but he had white shoes. He was wearing brown pants and a white shirt and he had a bowler balanced on his head and his hair was messy. And he was wearing a vest; two vests, maybe three. It seemed he always put on more than one. And there he was walking toward the performers area to the right of the main stage at the Philadelphia Folk Festival.

Often at a folk festival, you see people like myself, walking with all sorts of things strapped across their shoulders. Instruments, gig bags, cases of albums; hauling all your stuff to the festival site. And I've seen famous people with entourages surrounding them wherever they went. And I've seen these same sorts of famous people with hoards of fans coming up to look at them or to touch them or to ask them for an autograph, or some other sort of affirmation.

But there was John walking across the field all by himself. He was taking little steps and walking towards the performers area, and he seemed to be in a hurry. It's a long way from where the shuttle drops you off to the performers area, maybe a couple hundred yards. But there he was walking.

And I found myself walking towards him. I thought about going over to meet him, to say hello, but I stopped and just watched. I realized it would take a long time for him to walk that entire distance at his current pace. I watched for just a little longer and went off to find something to eat.

After supper, I wound my way around the back of the big main stage area and got into the performers area. I don't remember how much time passed since I first saw John walking, but by the time I had my supper and got to the performers area, he was there. And he had his fiddle out of the case and he was playing.

John had brought his string band with him for this trip to Philadelphia. Mike Compton, the fine mandolin player was there. And so was the young man whose name I've forgotten, who plays guitar. He wears an old-time hat and he backs up John on the guitar. He plays a big old Martin and uses a thumb pick the same way Mother Maybelle Carter did. I want to say his first name is Chris. He's a very tasteful musician, and he was there. Also, Bob Carlin was there, the clawhammer banjo player. Bob is originally from Philadelphia, and I once heard John call him, "The only Yankee banjo player I'd ever play with." And Bob with banjo, and Chris with his guitar and Mike with his mandolin and John with his fiddle were all jamming in the performers area.

John was playing the one fiddle of his that has the scroll carved into the shape of a person's head and shoulders. As I remember, that fiddle was ornate, but not overly so. Like John, it was unique; a one-of-a-kind.

John was sitting there jaw cocked, his elbows up, bowler tilted on his head playing the fiddle, and the boys were picking right along. Some of the folks hanging around in the performers area had their instruments out. Some were just watching and listening, and some were quietly trying to play along, bewildered to find that John and the boys were picking in the key of E flat. John likes to play his fiddle music in keys other than the ones they're most often heard.

Some performers were there. I remember seeing Saul Brody, and he had his harmonica, and there were others whom I didn't recognize. And this lovely jam session began to unfold. There was no talking and there were no rules laid out. But it was in the key of E flat. If you could figure that out, you could get your instrument out of its case and tune it up right along with everybody.

It seemed apparent that John comes to these festivals to play music like this. I don't know how long it took for him to walk across that field, but I can't imagine he arrived as early as he did and walked that distance to sit and wait for something to happen.

I stood in a place where I could watch John play and still keep my eye on the rest of the circle. The music was good. It wasn't too fast, but it bounced along, right in the pocket. The fiddle, the mandolin and the banjo took turns picking the lead while the others settled into a comfortable groove.

John had been battling leukemia for the longest time, and I had known that he had recently been sick again. I decided to get my long neck Vega out of the bag, and I tuned it up to E flat. I went back and joined the circle and the group was playing a new one, "The Soldier's Joy." But by the time I entered the circle, it wasn't "The Soldier's Joy" anymore. Fiddle tune players and banjo players who play fiddle tunes always start with the melody, and then they begin taking it apart. They embellish it, and they change it. They add things to it, and they add themselves to it. And then they take things out again. The instrumentalists were playing and twisting that simple melody this way and that, entertaining themselves and each other with new inventions and variations on a tune each has probably known his entire life.

So by the time I entered the circle again with my long neck banjo, the tune being played wasn't really "The Soldier's Joy" anymore, only the chord progression of the tune being played could be called, "The Soldier's Joy."

I took the chair to John's left. I watched him, and I chunked along with the rhythm. John had laid out for a time and let some of the other boys play. He was under that bowler, jaw cocked, expressionless, eyes watching things, plucking the rhythm out on his fiddle with his thumb. A bystander may have guessed he was half asleep, but I do believe he was very alert. This is how music gets played when John's around. He was watching and listening to everybody. And "The Soldier's Joy" was pouring out of those instruments.

Saul Brody was standing on the other side of John wearing his cowboy hat. Pretty soon, John reached over with his fiddle bow and tapped him on the shin. That must of meant it was Saul's turn to play. The boys looked at Saul and their backing was polite and solid; maybe they were glad somebody else was going to do the work for awhile and Saul seized his moment. He blew a most intricate and beautiful thirty-two bars, and left a little of himself in the version of "The Soldier's Joy" this group of strangers had been fashioning out of the thin air that summer afternoon in eastern Pennsylvania.

John kept thumbing the rhythm on his fiddle as one of the boys picked up on Saul's solo. The music surged a little bit on Saul's energy, and the boys and the rest of us hung on as a new crispness settled into the rhythm. Around and around the tune went, to banjo, over to someone else on the fiddle, then over to the mandolin, then some young fellow who tried to pick hot on his guitar, then Saul again. All the while John kept thumbing the rhythm on his fiddle watching and listening. As the tune wound down on the current pass, John stopped thumbing and cocked the fiddle under his jaw. He drew back the bow, and his fiddle drawled and bubbled and sang and soared. I watched him play, still chording along on the rhythm. John finished up and went back to thumbing. Someone else picked up on the tune, and that's when it dawned on me.

I had been playing the banjo up to that point for twenty years. Twenty years I had been playing the banjo, and I had known "The Soldier's Joy" from almost the beginning. Since then I had been playing it straight, taking it apart, adding things of my own, taking things from other people and adding them and throwing things out to make room for still others. And it dawned on me that afternoon at the Philadelphia Folk Festival, the summer before John Hartford died, that never once had I asked myself the question, "How would I play 'The Soldier's Joy' if were I sitting next to John Hartford?"

And then it happened. John's fiddle bow no longer dangled as his thumb brushed the chords. He held it firm in his hand and drew it forward, towards me. He didn't look at me, but his fiddle bow touched my knee as if he were brushing away a fly. I looked at him and the words, "Play, son," came out of his mouth. It was my turn, and I realized that this was the exact wrong time to be asking the question first formulated a few moments earlier.

I didn't know what to do, but the time was here. I picked up the tune as the last pass ended and was nervous; thinking too much. I did get a a good piece of the melody started and thought I'd just stay with that. After the initial burst of excitement, the melody to "The Soldier's Joy" came washing back inside my ear and soon ran down through my arms to the fingertips working the banjo neck. The second A part started, and I began to settle in some.

My notes were a little more articulate, and the authority started to come back to my right arm, and I started feeling good. I thought to try and play it as simply and as straightforward as I possibly could.

"Whoosh," went the strings, and a good roll got the B part started. I whipped up those high notes on the first string and double-thumbed right on through to the second B part, ending my pass with the little flourish I have used to end "The Soldier's Joy" ever since I can remember.

Someone picked up the tune, and I eased back a little in my chair. I settled again into the rhythm, and my heart was pounding. I thought I did okay. After a time I looked again at John.

Expressionless, he thumbed along on his fiddle with the bouncing tempo. Two A parts went by and then two B's. John again cocked the fiddle back under his chin and raised up his bow one more time. I looked at the way his jaw was set against the fiddle. I looked at the way his hat was tilted on his head, wisps of gray hair spilling out from under the brim. I looked at his eyes and they were far away. We were far away. How many times had I sat like this and played myself into this same trance? And I wondered how many more times John had done the same.

In that moment I remembered again how he walked across the field earlier in the day. I could see again how slowly he walked, yet how much in a hurry he was. And I remembered again, how nobody in the circle had said a word, how we just played and reached out for one another and allowed good music to happen. And it seemed at that moment, as it has seemed to me ever since, that music like this is no more and no less than an ongoing conversation between hearts.

As daylight faded on the big field at the Philadelphia Folk Festival, it seemed then as if "The Soldier's Joy" had always been there. It seemed as if it had no real beginning and that it has no end. It seemed at that time, as if "The Soldier's Joy" and all the other tunes are always around us and everywhere, going along somewhere beneath the routines of daily life. And they appear again when the instruments are in tune, and when the folks sitting in the circle wish for them to arrive again.

I was still looking at John's eyes when his bow touched the fiddle strings.

And then he winked at me.

Folk songs are full of life.
They are the rhythm of work,
and the sweat rolling down your back
and off your brow.

Folk songs are the hurt of love unreturned
and the ache of being a long, weary way from home
for too long a time.

Folk songs are squinting, sunburned eyes,
scanning some far-off horizon,
looking for a way,
beyond the hills and trees and rivers.

Folk songs are a glint of humor
glancing off hard times and trouble.

Folk songs are a balmy breeze coming in from the south
on a warm morning.

Folk songs are a long and winding story
of a young hero you never met,
but somehow always knew.

Folk songs are remembering the people
from whom you have learned.

Singing folk songs marks a trail, another may follow.

Folk songs are full of life.

North Platte, Nebraska

The terrain surrounding North Platte is that of the West, not the Midwest. The sky is huge and the spaces beneath wide open. It is Nebraska, but feels like Wyoming. I checked twice, it is Nebraska. The cottonwoods look dry, but the hills are still green and lush. Though they have a lot of corn out here, the farmers somehow look more like ranchers. What we call cows in Illinois are called cattle out here.

On the way to North Platte, grain elevators are the first structures to appear on the horizon. And one can see a summer storm blowing through far off in the distance. The pace is slower out here, the drivers faster. The rivers are flat and muddy and pretty in their own way. It is windy all the time, and the terrain takes on a kind of ruggedness. Thankfully, the North Platte Wal-Mart restored some continuity to my eroding Midwestern sensibilities. It looked like all the other Wal-Marts. The people looked like all the other Wal-Mart people.

Earlier in the day I got a haircut in Lincoln, which is a pleasant city. Lincoln is home to the University of Nebraska and the state Capitol. Lincoln seems less industrial than the parts of Omaha I have seen, which makes a kind of sense. There is an immense football stadium downtown and there are what looks like a couple of nice museums too. Sculptures are sprinkled around the downtown area.

I got coffee in a funky coffeehouse on P street. The woman who cut my hair and the woman who served my coffee were each young and pretty and pleasant. Leaving the coffee shop and walking around the corner off P Street, a car accident had taken place shortly before my arrival. The man and woman involved in the accident were talking to each other in pleasant tones, even though their vehicles were damaged and their passengers shaken. They looked like nice people, and Lincoln, Nebraska seems as pleasant a place as any to have a car accident.

With my haircut and coffee, I was back in the truck and wound myself out of town through some beautiful country, along Route 6. West of Lincoln, Route 6 hooks up with Route 34 near a town called Hastings. Hastings is just this side of another town called Minden. Thirty years ago, almost to the day, I spent a night in a cornfield along Route 34 somewhere near Minden.

Not long out of high school, a friend and I had spent an entire summer on our motorcycles. We swam in both oceans, hiked a short piece of the Appalachian trail and discovered the Rockies for the first time. We wandered up Route One in California, spent a short time - a very short time - in a hippie commune, climbed a small mountain in Big Sur on our own, looked for Neil Young's ranch outside San Francisco, slept in a cabin across the lake from Mt. St. Helens, loved the green wetness of the Great Northwest, spent a ponderous afternoon hiking the grounds of the Little Big Horn, and I found out just how fast a Yamaha 650 twin can go with the wind in Wyoming. And on and on like that.

What turned out to be our last night on the road, 68 days in all if I remember right, was spent in a somber mood by a cornfield near Minden, Nebraska. We had crisscrossed our way south from Montana through the Grand Tetons again, and the Rockies. We camped for three nights in Rocky Mountain National Park and got drunk on Coors Beer in Estes Park. At last we aimed our bikes toward home as money and time were running out. The exhilaration of the mountains flattened with the terrain of eastern Colorado. We pushed ahead for two more rambling days, heading back north, then south again, looking still for something that might spark our interest one more time before the final, inevitable day.

And that day turned out to be somewhere near Minden, at a roadside table along Route 34. I don't remember what we ate, perhaps a pizza in some town earlier in the day. Perhaps some edible canned food of one kind or another, but I don't remember a fire that night. I remember a tree and a picnic table. I remember Nebraska corn so tall you could hide in it standing up. I remember the blackest of nights and stars like we had never seen. I remember hair down past my shoulders bleached blonde with the sun of many summer days spent out-of-doors. I remember the skin on my face and skinny arms had turned to rich bronze, my nose pink and scabbed with sunburn.

We carried no tent that summer. Just the clothes on our backs, an extra shirt and sleeping bag, a couple of groundcloths each, a notebook, a camera, a jacket with lots of pockets, a guitar and more tools than we needed. Our strategy was to sleep for free when possible. As it turned out, we spent a number of nights in places we probably weren't supposed to be. We were good kids and intended no trouble. We thought others would permit our gentle passing through as our youth and goodness were surely evident. And so it was at the roadside table somewhere near Minden.

We had devised a system of shelter should the weather become inclement. The bikes were to be parked one at each end of a picnic table, and through some construction of ground cloth and bungee cord, a suitable shelter would be struck complete with central heating from the warmth of two motorcycle engines.

We spent some rainy days that summer, but never once slept in the rain the entire trip. In the West you can see the storms coming. It was fun dodging rain clouds out where the storms tend to blow through in a hurry. It was fun changing plans with the turn of a handlebar.

We had wished to prove to ourselves, I guess, that two young bucks could stay dry and happy beneath a picnic table for an entire summer, laughing off rain and the cruel world, while paying no rent. We ate modestly, and in one summer drank in by large gulps, a glimpse of a world that until such time we had only heard about through rumor and lore. The product of all of this I suppose, was an initiation of sorts; a self-initiation. I had hoped for epiphany, but remember mostly traffic jams, hoards of frazzled vacationers, annoyed park rangers, loneliness, fatigue, cops, many wonderful people and more than a few weirdos. I remember my friend and I being at odds over the most trivial matters. Not only things like tuning motorcycle engines, but we also had arguments over thousand island dressing and the best way to change flashlight batteries.

Thirty years later, I still have trivial arguments with friends and traveling partners. And off in the corners, I still hear about that same wondrous world my friend and I were first called to explore. Things change they do. I am no longer free to make plans by the turn of a handlebar. And storms no longer seem to blow through in a hurry. Dinty Moore stew does not a supper make, nor does Underwood Deviled Ham on Wonder Bread. Coors no longer counts as beer, and I haven't been on a motorcycle since the last time I fell off of one and got hurt.

I do remember though, that last night near Minden as if it were yesterday. I remember lying there, looking up at the stars past the silhouettes of tall corn stalks. How beautiful and endless the stars seemed, and still seem. I've never forgotten them. I remember the velvet sound of cornstalks rustling with the night breeze, and I remember how sleep was slow to come. I remember the soft earth beneath my bag, and I remember wondering why we had never slept in a cornfield before. The earth in a cornfield makes a lovely mattress.

We had toted a guitar along with us the entire trip. I learned my first chords the year before and played guitar almost every day on that trip. We sang by ourselves and with others in all the campgrounds. I remember thinking before sleep on that final night that I would resolve to study guitar when I got home. I resolved that night to enroll in classes at the Old Town School of Folk Music in Chicago when the new session began in the fall..

Going home, and going home to the rest of our lives, was of course inevitable. And I thought maybe these stars and this west, perhaps a piece of this freedom and maybe even this whole summer might last forever if I worked at the guitar and mastered it some. That's what I thought. College was no longer an option, only the guitar would do. The guitar after that summer, was cemented forever to my future.

And this afternoon, no rest area along Route 34 could I find. No picnic table, no tree. I turned around twice and drove both east and west of Minden. I followed 34 far further each way than I had intended and spent more time looking than I should have. I saw a few places where it might have once been, but it was hard to tell. There were new houses here and there and all I could do was wonder.

This afternoon I had hoped to close a circle that first opened up that starlit night, thirty summers ago. I had hoped to sit on that same picnic table, under that same tree and listen again to the rustling stalks in that same cornfield. I was hoping to get a clear look at and feel for, the thing that thirty years represents. Not to be.

I did stop at one place. It wasn't *the* place, but I felt I had to stop somewhere. I pulled off 34 and turned up a dirt road headed northeast. I parked about 50 yards in and dropped the tailgate of my truck. Cottonwoods shimmered in the wind. I opened a Pepsi and sat on the tailgate and ate some pretzels and a peach. I thought again about that summer with Tim on our motorcycles, and at some point I laughed. After a time I walked around behind the truck to take a pee and noticed my new haircut in the reflection of the side window. Through the glass were my guitars and banjos packed in their cases and stowed in the back with all the other gear for a short summer tour. A semi whined out on the highway. Across the way an ocean of sunlit cornstalks swayed. I finished my Pepsi, checked the map and thought I might make North Platte by suppertime.

An Unsent Letter

It's cold for November. The weather report was calling for snow, and by the time my concert ended this afternoon and the truck was packed, the sky had grown overcast and the air was heavy and frozen. It is good to be finally heading home. The last ten days were good though; New Jersey, Delaware and Springfield, Massachusetts. The shows were well attended, and I sang and played reasonably well. The audience at the Springfield Fine Arts Museum was especially energetic and refreshing. Lots of kids and families. It was fun to get them singing along and engaged in music and laughter.

Leaving Springfield, I headed west up through the Berkshires towards New York, towards home, and I remembered James Taylor singing about this very turnpike in his song, "Sweet Baby James." It seems like I have heard "Sweet Baby James" thousands of times by now. In bars and on jukeboxes, on the radio and plenty of times on my own record player. I've taught it to many, many students over the years, who slogged through the weird chord changes; none of whom could hold it in when the chorus came around. I remembered how sweetly I once heard James sing it in concert. The song seemed to want to wrap the whole hall and the whole weary world up in some warm memory and rock us all to sleep, cozy and happy.

James sang about the Berkshires and how dreamlike they seemed in the snow. How dreamlike the Berkshires seemed this afternoon when the sun winked its last, and disappeared behind the high hills somewhere upstate New York, and November's weird low light glanced and finally faded, leaving silhouettes where there once were trees and houses and mountains. The shadows rolled in long and dark and evening haze began to appear and rise above the river bottoms and across the blue horizon.

And then, while driving, there was this moment when I noticed my heartbeat. I heard it first in my ears, then felt it pulse down my neck and jaw and finally felt it in my chest. Tum-tumm, tum-tumm. While watching the headlights reach into the darkness, I noticed too the gentle rise and fall of my breathing. It of course, had been there all along, but now it entered my awareness like the second movement of some quiet symphony. I could feel and hear the little wisps of air being drawn and pushed through my sinus and mouth and nose. It was delicate. It was ballet.

Maybe the road does this to you. Sitting quietly mile after mile, day after day. Eating alone, thinking all the time and conversing with only yourself and those who are mostly strangers. It's sometimes hard. But you do get to sing.

I was happy and settled while listening to and feeling the little dance a body does when it is alive. I wasn't thinking about being hungry or tired or worried about how many more miles there were left to drive. I listened for and felt the moment when a single breath began, and when that same breath was finished. And then a new one. Tum-tumm, tum-tumm. Then I heard the motor of the truck strike a groan as we pitched into the rising terrain of the Catskills. The truck shifted gears, and the motor wound out some as we climbed. I left my listening to watch the road and negotiate the curves and traffic that had appeared from out of nowhere.

When the road had flattened again, and the cars and trucks were all gone, and the dark and quiet returned, I tried once more to listen for my heartbeat; to listen for and feel my breathing. My heartbeat and breathing were still there of course. But the moment was no longer. Thoughts of work and home, and scenes from the last week crashed in and clamored about, replaying themselves in an odd and boisterous montage of images, faces and sounds.

Again I thought about the Berkshires and about James. I thought about music and songs. I thought about my guitar and my banjo and how long they have been giving me a living. I thought about my new record, and I thought about Frank and the simple magic that is around us all the time. I thought about the Old Town School and my students. I thought about you.

And from somewhere I began to sing. I felt my mouth form the words and the tune was good. It rose up out of my dry throat and across my lips, and I tried to make it sound a little like the sweetness I remembered the first time I heard James sing.

"There is a young cowboy..."

Slaughterhouse Five Steak Salad

"We are here on earth to fart around and don't let anybody tell you any different," said writer Kurt Vonnegut, Jr. It was rainy and cold the day Kurt Vonnegut, Jr. died, almost two years ago to the day. I'd come home from a gig in the late afternoon hungry and somehow disturbed by the news. His son Mark would later say, describing the event that led to his father's passing, "Kurt fell, hit his head, and irreversibly scrambled his precious egg."

Famous people and the unknown alike acknowledge a feeling of gratitude for Kurt and his work. His novels and essays are at once literary and satirical. Some of his stories resemble science fiction and a basis for humor simmers throughout almost everything he wrote. Kurt could make people laugh. Those of us who have read him and have heard him speak and have carried his wisdom and humor into the depths of personal dilemma share a unique kinship.

Kurt was not a young man by the time he left earth. He was into his eighties and a chain smoker. When he complained about having lived so long, his son Mark told him that God was curious about how many cigarettes a human being could smoke, and He couldn't help wondering what was going to come out of his mouth next.

And I found myself oddly troubled while preparing supper that night. I recalled over the years, reading and rereading his novels. I recalled the time, towards the end of his life, hearing him speak and getting to shake his hand.

"I am very pleased to meet you," I said. He seemed a little annoyed with having to meet so many people, but his eyes were loving.

"Thank you," he said. And he smiled, his craggy face creased with the lines of one who smiled often.

Before the days of the internet, I remember going to libraries in different places, particularly where there was a university, to look up criticisms of his work. I wanted to understand him better. I wanted to figure out how he made me laugh. I wanted to know how his stories had helped me learn to keep thinking and wondering. And hoping.

I miss Kurt a little, even though we met just once. Every so often I go back and revisit a dog-eared Vonnegut paperback, or pull a hardcover from the shelf. I like a quiet afternoon with a good book. I have tapes of him reading his work and they are great. And I practice my own writing more regularly now. I read it out loud, just as he suggested, listening for syntax and diction, and listening further for clarity and a balance of sarcasm. These have become my humble parameters for good prose. These were Kurt's parameters too, but in a much more sublime and magnificent way.

So it goes, as Kurt might say. Here is the recipe for my supper the evening Kurt Vonnegut passed away. By far, it is my most famous salad so I named it after his most famous novel. I tried it once in the summer with grilled chicken and ranch dressing and it was okay. But I only made it that way the one time.

SLAUGHTERHOUSE FIVE STEAK SALAD with CREAM of MUSHROOM SOUP
Ingredients

- ½ lb to 1 lb steak of choice
- 8 oz portobello mushrooms
- 1 good sized roma tomato
- medium sized red pepper
- four stalks romaine lettuce

- two big handfuls of baby spinach leaves
- Wishbone Original Western dressing
- crumbles of bleu cheese
- 1 can Campbell's Cream of Mushroom Soup
- 8 ounces whole milk
- 1 bottle merlot or pinot noir
- serves two

Preparation

1) Take the steak out of the package and let it sit on the counter, uncovered for one hour. Rib Eye is my favorite. New York Strip is great. Ranch steak or skirt steak will also serve well. Sirloin is only okay.

2) Open the bottle of wine and pour a glass. Pour two glasses if there are two of you.

3) Preheat the oven to 250 degrees.

4) Chop the stems off the portobellos and put them aside. Slice the buttons and separate them into two piles, placing one pile along with the stems.

5) Core and stem the red pepper and cut it in half. Slice each half into thin long strips and set aside.

6) Put a fire under one cast iron skillet until it is pretty hot. Pour in a tablespoon of olive oil or canola oil and let it heat up some. Then add a tablespoon of butter or margarine. When it melts down, throw in the pile of portobellos with the stems. These are for the soup. Saute to taste.

7) Open the can of soup and glop it into a sauce pan. Pepper it. Add 4 ounces milk and put under low heat, mixing until combined.

Pepper it again. When the initial glop and milk are combined and peppered, add 4 more ounces of milk and the sauteed portobellos. Pepper again. Keep stirring.

8) Prepare the skillet as before and put the remaining portobellos in. These are for the salad. Saute to taste, then put aside.

9) Liberally sprinkle kosher salt all over your steak. Then grind some fresh pepper all over it too.

10) Now wipe out the portobello skillet (careful, it's still hot). Now heat it up again until it becomes as hot as a branding iron. Pour in two tablespoons of canola or safflower oil. When the pan and oil are heated, open the kitchen door to give the smoke somewhere to go. Add a big glob of margarine or butter and when it's melted down some, place the steak in the pan. Liberally sprinkle kosher salt and pepper on the unseasoned side of the steak.

11) In about two minutes, flip the steak over. It ought to be brown and crusty. Yum.

12) Halve a Roma tomato and then slice each half into segments.

13) In a second iron skillet (a wok is better), throw in the sliced red peppers without any oil. heat them until crisp and blackened. Take them out. You may want to throw the portobellos in also, just to heat them up again.

14) Take the skillet with the steak off the heat and put it in the oven. I often cut the steak in half to see the beautiful sear and the undercooked center. This gives me an idea of how long it might have to remain in the oven. Remember, that's a hot skillet and

the meat is hot and still cooking. Five minutes in the oven is a long time. But let it in there until you're happy with it. Medium rare is the chef's recommendation.

15) Break up the romaine stalks and place the pieces into a salad bowl or dish. Place a big handful of baby spinach leaves on top with artful purpose. Do this for both dishes, you're serving two.

16) Place the blackened red pepper slices around the outer edge of each salad dish. Place the tomato segments inside the ring of red pepper slices equidistantly.

17) When the steak is done to order, slice into thin strips and let stand. Pour a circle of Wishbone Original Western dressing about the ring of blackened red pepper and roma tomato slices.

18) Place 4 - 8 slices of meat across each bed of spinach leaves. Place a portion of sauteed portobellos atop the meat slices.

19) Sprinkle crumbled bleu cheese atop the portobellos and meat.

20) Ladle out a serving of mushroom soup. I like mine in a tea cup. Add more pepper.

21) Enjoy.

Weary Prodigal Come

Pohjanmaan kautta means "Cheers!" in Finland, and I am wondering how to say it. Is it po-SZHYAN-mahn? Or PO-john-man? Is it KAW-ta?

I looked it up online and learned the more literal translation is "down the hatch," which I haven't heard in any language in a long time. The last time may have been on a Three Stooges episode I saw when I was a kid.

I am honored then, to represent the Old Town School of Folk Music along with my colleagues Colby Maddox and Dr. Paul Tyler for a whirlwind tour of Finland as part of Bau Graves' international faculty exchange program. We three are being billed as DMT (pronounced Moe, Larry, Curly). Bassist John Abbey will also be joining us for the shows, and we are mighty glad of it. Everybody knows there were really four Stooges.

Here's what I know about Finland so far: In June, it is daylight almost the whole time. In Finland, it is unmannerly to wear your BVD's in the sauna. In Finland, they eat a lot of fish. And reindeer. Helsinki is the largest city and is only 437 miles from the Arctic Circle. That's roughly the distance between Chicago and Dover, Tennessee, where I met a retired tobacco farmer at a music festival last week. Though he acknowledged having been north of Paducah, Kentucky only twice in his entire lifetime, he cautioned me to be careful around the women in Finland. He also said it's cold there.

I am looking forward to meeting our hosts Juha and Wasel. I am excited about the chance to play and sing with Colby, Paul and John, all of whom are excellent musicians and dedicated instructors. We've rehearsed well over the last six weeks or so and have found some musically exciting common ground. We're a little bluegrass, a little old-timey and somewhat folky. "Just good" is what I would say. That's *vain hyva* in Finland.

WEARY PRODIGAL COME
from the Carter Family

God is calling the prodigal "Come without delay"
Hear oh hear him calling, calling now for thee
Patient, loving and tender lie still the Father's plea
Hear His loving voice calling still

Calling out for thee
Weary prodigal come, weary prodigal come
Calling out for thee
Oh weary prodigal come, weary prodigal come

Come there's bread in the house of the Father and to spare
Hear oh hear him calling, calling now for thee
Lo and the table is spread and the feast is waiting there
Hear His loving voice calling still

Calling out for thee
Weary prodigal come, weary prodigal come
Calling out for thee
Oh weary prodigal come, weary prodigal come.

Yesterday I Was Baptized

Yesterday I was baptized. I awoke in the late afternoon with a full blown case of jet lag. My throat was scratchy, my sinuses dry, and I had the same feeling of congestion in my chest that precedes something like a flu. There was laughter and music coming from Colby and Paul's apartment across the foyer. First one mandolin then two together. More laughter. One voice was thick with the speaking style common to these northern regions, the other more familiar. Names were being mentioned, and I only recognized a few. Someone unschooled in mandolin nobility is left then, to measure the magnitude of each name by only the reverence with which it is spoken.

Wasel Arar and Colby Maddox were jamming and comparing notes collected from two separate lifetimes spent bent over a mandolin in two completely different parts of the world. And to recognize how much they have found in common with one another is something to behold. Some of the same chops and riffs spill out of their instruments. They share some of the same chord voicings and scales, as well as a number of common musical friendships in the swirling world known only to those who pick at the mandolin. Details like string gauges, action, model numbers beginning with an A or an F, were discussed and affirmed. Builders like Gibson and Kentuckian and others I have never heard of were addressed.

I made tea in the kitchen of John's and my apartment, enjoying the interaction. It is evident that Wasel loves all kinds of music. He is quick to point out some of the many things old-time music and bluegrass have in common. It is remarkable that Wasel has learned to play so well and has amassed so much knowledge considering the essence of his music is rooted a half a world away. He knows instruments too. He knows how they are built and how they ought to be adjusted. And he can articulate the subtle differences in the sound of one mandolin when compared to the next. I gathered then that Wasel has listened to a great many mandolins.

Now let me tell you something else. Sitting in my kitchen sipping tea, I thought I heard lightning sparking from the strings of Colby Maddox. His playing is at once powerful, subtle and rhythmic. His phrasing dances and struts with bluesy, syncopated vigor. Whoa.

I boiled another cup of tea water and listened to the music a while longer, then joined the two in the other apartment. "I am taking you all to the sauna this afternoon," said Wasel. The word *sauna* hung in the air. *Sow-nah.* I guess you could say Colby and I said nothing, as it suddenly became awful quiet. "You'll enjoy it," Wasel went on, "It is something you come to Finland to do. All Finns enjoy their *sauna.*"

Twenty minutes later, the four of us plus Wasel trudged down the gravel road, towels draped over our shoulders, towards sauna. *Sow-nah.* Wasel explained some of the health giving benefits of this age old Finnish tradition as we walked. He was eager for us to take part in the experience, yet sensitive to the shyness of his American guests. I wondered how many American musicians Wasel has coaxed and coached through their first Finnish sauna over the years. *Sow-nah.*

At once Wasel stopped in mid-sentence. "Wait a minute," he said, "I forgot something. Keep on walking and I'll catch up with you." The four of us kept on towards our sauna. John, who has traveled the world playing music, has enjoyed sauna in several different countries. Paul is generally eager to try new things and although this wouldn't be his first sauna, he was fully looking forward to it. I'm pretty sure Colby and I said nothing, as it again became awful quiet.

Wasel came hustling up the road toting a twelve pack carton of Finnish beer. "We'll need these in the sauna," he said.

We entered what Wasel called the dressing room, which is an interesting thing to call it, and we began undressing. "You can take your towel in if you like," said Wasel. "You are all welcome to do what you are comfortable with. But if you take your towel in, it will get wet and you won't have anything to dry yourself off with."

As we stood, one of the boys handed me an open bottle of beer. I folded my towel and placed it atop my stack of clothing, and we exited the dressing room. Across the hall is the doorway to the sauna. As you enter you step past a container about the size of a small trash can. It is filled with what look to be man-made stones which are somehow heated by the container. Two gents, already sweating and pink welcomed us. We stepped up one at a time, and the older of the two scootched around the u-shaped bench to make room. The younger one stayed on the end nearest the container and manned the pail. Periodically he splashed a ladleful of water atop the rocks. The water sizzled and evaporated, filling the sauna with heat and moisture.

A Finnish sauna is rather compact and is hotter than a traffic jam in Louisiana in August. Eighty degrees centigrade is a hundred seventy-six in our part of the world, and you feel it immediately. Wasel explained something of the philosophy behind sauna. He spoke something in Finnish to the younger man who immediately splashed two more ladles of water on the stones. The water sizzled again and the heat increased.

"There is an art to sauna," Wasel explained. "You have to do things slowly, and when you feel it is time, we will step out back to the river."

Soon enough the time came. Dripping with sweat, we tiptoed out of the sauna down the short hall and tiptoed out of the doorway which led to the river. There we paused for a spell, and I ducked back to the dressing room to deposit my empty bottle. While there I heard Wasel calling something to the others, and by the time I came back out, John, Colby and Paul were already in the water. "Some people like to dive right in," Wasel said to me, "but try easing in and see how you like it. You may find it easier to back down the ladder into the water." I turned around facing Wasel and backed down the ladder.

The water was cold but not icy. Steam was coming off my arms and off of Wasel's shoulders. "Watch your step he said, the ladder is slippery." I was in about as far as my knees and looked down to make certain my feet were steady on the ladder. I felt Wasel's hand atop my head. He mumbled, "I hearby baptize you into the river of *sauna*," and he pushed. I pushed off the ladder with my legs and fell back laughing into the chilly water. Wasel stepped down the ladder and joined us. "Don't be in a hurry to get out of the water," he said. "You'll know when it's time."

One carries the heat of the sauna into the river with him. And the heat of the sauna remains when one climbs back up the ladder and out of the water. Colby and John fetched another round of bottles from the dressing room, and there we stood, talking and drinking, watching dusk and stillness settle on the lagoon. A seagull screeched from her perch on a rock while her still fuzzy babies paddled in the water below.

Finnish sauna is refreshing, just as Wasel promised, and invigorating. The shyness of disrobing in public is only temporary. Sauna in Finland is as commonplace as cell phones are in Lincoln Square, and one falls into the custom quite naturally. While fully clothed and facing an audience, I have felt more naked on countless other occasions, with guitar in hand and a good set list to boot. *Sownah.*

Colby began to shiver, and I began to shiver. The process of heating up in the sauna and cooling off in the river can be repeated as many times as one prefers. Wasel recommended three, so three it was. Paul and Colby stayed for a fourth, while John and I showered, dressed and headed over to the restaurant for dinner. The room was crowded and by the time we arrived, a bluegrass jam had already assembled in the corner. We took the small table by the door and ordered, astonished to find out it was nine thirty. We had spent more than two and a half hours in the sauna.

Can You Tell Me Which Way is North?

Elovena is a kind of instant breakfast cereal. We've been calling it "porridge," which somehow seems appropriate so long as we are in Finland. Elovena is produced by the Hetki Company and only requires some boiling water and one minute of your time. There is a graphic on the box of a lovely Finnish lass in her peasant dress and bonnet, and she is carrying a bundle of wheat and looking out across the table directly at me. There are some red things in my Elovena, which resemble bits of dehydrated berries, and I have chopped and loaded on the other half of yesterday's banana and a half an apple.

My throat is better today, and my sinus has improved. I feel more rested than at any time I can remember over the last month and that is a good thing. The sun is out and it is warmer. We are scheduled to participate in a concert at the church at noon today, and we are scheduled to entertain in the saloon at the Wild West Village later today, also a kind of church. Familiar images of the American West have somehow taken root here and been reborn a curious hybrid of culture and stereotype.

It is a beautiful morning in the town where I am, though I am still unsure of its name or where it is located. I have devised an impish little game for the purpose of my own entertainment, and it goes like this: I will be walking and encounter another passerby. If our eyes meet, I wave. If he or she waves back or acknowledges my gesture, I pause and ask, "Excuse me, can you tell me which way is north?"

Sometimes the language barrier is too much. One guy tried to give me money. Most other times the guy will stop and look at the sky and then the tree line and point in this direction or that. I have pulled this ruse successfully perhaps a half-dozen times while here in the village whose-name-I-can't-pronounce, and standing in front of the restaurant across the street from the lagoon, I can now point you north in six different directions.

We are making do in our little duplex. On day one I blew the fuse on my adapter trying to recharge camera batteries and have bungled many attempts at trying to access the internet with some ethernet rig Wasel has lent us for our stay. I have endured two cold showers before figuring out how to turn on the water heater and made a disaster of trying to operate the Mocha Master, a thing they call a coffee maker here in Finland. I have lost three flatpicks and broken one string. The battery in my tuner died in the cold while on stage yesterday afternoon, and then after I put in a new one, the whole thing died in the cold during our pub show last night at the restaurant. I wound up giving it to a boy who was perhaps ten years old. I asked him if he could point in the direction that is north. Without hesitation he pointed straight up to the sky, by far the best answer yet, so I figured he deserved a prize.

Coffee All Day

I awoke this morning a few minutes before the travel alarm was set to go off. John was already in the shower and sunlight poured through the transom window of our tiny room at Hotel Helka, turning a big swatch of the south wall golden yellow. Steam from the coffee maker on the desk drifted upward, casting a delicate, swirling shadow upon the wall. The coffeepot was one cup shy of full and although just beyond the foot of my bed, it seemed an entire ocean away.

It is getaway day in Helsinki, and at some point I will crawl out from beneath the covers. In a few moments my feet will hit the floor, I will head towards the bathroom where John is now humming something beneath the drone of the hair dryer, and the long journey toward home will have begun. John's humming and the drone of the hair dryer conclude simultaneously, the door squeaks open and he appears, ready to get moving.

"Morning Mark," he says, "Can I pour you a coffee?"

Knowing full well he doesn't need an answer, John tips the pot to the rim of a styrofoam cup. I sit up a little and he hands it to me. It is hotel room coffee, but it is good. And it is hot.

"I hope you don't mind," John says, "I borrowed some of your Barbasol. That's great stuff, I use it at home." And after a pause he adds, "And it's still only ninety-nine cents!"

Somehow the price of cheap shaving cream made us laugh. This sort of chat is the kind of nonsense that helps to sustain travelers like we. It's a way to agree upon an acceptable mood for the day and a way to measure perspective. Loneliness and worry don't come knocking so long as there's a little work to do and a lot of nonsense to participate in. We four have covered thousands of miles over the last nine days, and the amount of actual time spent making music has been small when compared to the amount of time spent doing everything else - riding in planes and cars, reading, walking, talking, shopping, eating, typing, thinking, lying awake at night and making fun of ourselves and different bits and pieces of our curious shared adventure. One learns to look forward to the nonsense.

"I'm headed down to check the internet," said John. "I'll see you down there."

The breakfast buffet at Hotel Helka was good, but the coffee in our room was better. After breakfast, I rode the elevator back up to gather my bags and instruments. Once returned to the lobby, I plopped my well-fed, weary bones deep into a soft arm chair. I looked out the window, looked at the internet and kept a tired eye on the comings and goings at the reception desk. A little after seven, Colby, looking sleepy, appeared with all his stuff. We chatted for a bit and he ambled off towards the buffet, leaving me to look after his things.

In due time the cab would come and whisk Colby, John and me to the Helsinki airport. Paul was headed back to Sweden for some other business and I'm sure some more fiddle playing. And bless the remarkable woman behind the hotel desk who checked us out, who brought the coffeepot over to top off our cups while the Finnish bellhops loaded all our stuff into the van. Plastic lids appeared from her pocket, and the sleep-deprived folksingers enjoyed a spill-free trip to the airport.

There was time for a real coffee after our plane landed in Copenhagen for a five hour layover; after a private meeting with two customs agents who were curious about the tools in my bag, the pocket knife and the corkscrew. The one guy rooted around, discovered a jaw harp and held it up to the light asking me again and again what it was, never once giving me permission to play it for him. He finally allowed that I would have to check my backpack in with the other luggage, but I could keep my laptop, notebook, phone and my tattered paperback copy of Walt Whitman's *Leaves of Grass*.

John and Colby were already somewhere in the airport, and I headed over to a luggage boutique to buy a new shoulder bag. I found a good one which cost one hundred and forty-five Danish dollars. Later, I found out from the server at the cafe that a Danish dollar, a *krone,* is worth around seventeen American cents. So the bag cost about twenty-five bucks, and the coffee, served rich and black with raw sugar and thick cream on the side, cost around two seventy-five.

I opened my Whitman.

The earth never tires;
The earth is rude, silent, incomprehensible at first - Nature is
rude and incomprehensible at first;
Be not discouraged - keep on - there are divine things, well
enveloped;
I swear to you there are divine things more beautiful than words
can tell...

I bought this copy of *Leave of Grass* my senior year in high school and have carried it with me many places since then. The cover fell off a long time ago, and the pages are torn and marked and musty. Whitman is hard for me to read, but he carries something of the American essence that few have captured. And if I can stay with him long enough, his lines open up, and a glimpse of his beautiful vision will begin to appear. It's a kind of neat magic I have come to rely on over the years, especially so at times like this, when I am a long way from home and feeling unsettled. And so far, no iPhone app has yet been made available that will perform this feat so dependably.

I hear John call and I turn, and he says, "Did you make it through okay?"

"Everything's fine," I answer. "Where's Colby?"

"He's looking for some presents to bring home to his kids. Hey, do you want to hang around in the airport for the next five hours, or do you want to see if we can get downtown to Copenhagen and look around?"

Not thirty minutes later, we three were walking along cobblestone in historic Copenhagen. With the use of Colby's debit card, John had remarkably figured out how to produce three train tickets from a machine whose instructions included only obtuse pictures and words printed in Danish.

The history of Copenhagen dates back to the days of Vikings. It is a city of high culture and refinement, whose many churches, cathedrals, government buildings and museums strike a very kingly presence. Every few blocks is a sausage stand, where one can point to one of perhaps twenty different pictured menu items, hold out a pile of Danish coins, return to his pocket what the vendor has not removed, and be handed a delicious smelling thing on a roll that very much resembles a long American hot dog.

The downtown walking district of Copenhagen is a winding maze of shops, restaurants and cafes housed in what look to be very old buildings. No automobiles are allowed, and bicycles are everywhere. Though mimes, puppeteers and musicians add an element of festivity to the street atmosphere, the air remains sophisticated and urbane. We walkers and eaters and sightseers are an international community divided in half between those who are on their way to somewhere and the rest of us who are happy to lag along with the leisurely afternoon pace of this most elegant northern European city.

John picks out a bakery that offers tables on the street, a few of which are available. We order croissants and our server brings us each a half-liter pot of coffee. It is strong and good. The cream is fresh, the bakery delicate and lovely. John lights up a cigarette, and this strange wish to become a smoker suddenly makes itself apparent. And I do remember seeing a beret in the hat shop earlier on our walk.

After a time, Colby said, "We better be getting back. We don't want to miss our flight."

To get to Chicago from Copenhagen by air, one has to spend approximately nine hours on a plane. And those who have never done it before will learn that chasing the sun in an Airbus will lead to one very long day. We will touch down in Chicago sometime after three o'clock in the afternoon when my body will be thinking it is sometime after eleven at night. And who knows how long it will take to clear customs, retrieve my luggage, get to a train, walk over to Paul's house in the city where my car is parked, and navigate the gridlock of Chicago traffic back out to Riverside, Illinois.

The Soul travels; says Whitman.
The body does not travel as much as the soul;
The body has just as great a work as the soul, and parts away at
  last for the journey of the soul.
All parts away for the progress of souls;
All religion, all solid things, arts, governments, - all that was or is
  apparent upon this globe or any globe,
falls into niches and corners before the procession of Souls along

the grand roads of the universe...
Forever alive, forever forward,
Stately, solemn, sad, withdrawn, baffled, mad, turbulent, feeble,
 dissatisfied,
Desperate, proud, fond, sick, accepted by men, rejected by men,
They go! they go! I know that they go, but I know not where they
 go;
But I know that they go toward the best - toward something great.

"Excuse me," said the flight attendant, holding out a small bag of pretzels. "Would you like something to drink?"

"Yes," I say. "Coffee please. Black."

I am not yet awake
until I iron my shirt.
And slip my trousers on,
and fetch the work order
from the battered red ring binder
on the shelf.

I get my toll money from the dresser top
and gasoline from the Quick Mart
down the way.
I get a coffee to go,
and sometimes a newspaper,
before heading off somewhere
to play and sing
and laugh away an afternoon or evening
with some strangers
who have gathered a half-day's drive
from where I sleep
and take my messages;
from where I keep my messes
and piles of falling down laundry,
and books
and note pads scribbled full
with ideas not yet born.

I am not yet awake
until the radio on the dash is tuned
to the sports-talk station,
and I hear the groggy news of the home team,
and the jangle in the voices
of the call-in listeners.

And I am not yet awake
until I scan the dial
for some jazz,
or sing-along oldies,
or soothing strings,
or news,
should something be happening.

I am not yet awake
until I pull onto the highway
and merge with traffic,
cruising along,
cursing the slow-pokes
and speed demons
and ding-dongs;
all hustling off, like me,
to get somewhere on time,
to do their work,
to have their fun,
to collect their wages,
before heading back home.

And I am not yet awake
until I sip from my cup
and hang my elbow out the window,
and note how quickly
the wind and the world
are flying by.

I am not yet awake
until I park, not too far from the side door
of the hall or gymnasium,
or multi-purpose room,
and take off my cap
and check my hair in the rear-view mirror.

I am not yet awake
until I sling a banjo bag across my back
and a guitar case over my shoulder,
and walk to the door
making sure
I still have a purpose in mind.

I am not yet awake
until I say something nice
to the woman or man who greets me,
whether they are nice or not;
whether they are important or not.

I am not yet awake
until I get to the room
where I am to sing and play.
And taste the air
and notice the light
and listen
to those who have gathered and are waiting;
and I measure their buzzing
and hear their chatter
bouncing off the walls
and ceiling and curtains and tables.

I am not yet awake
until I find a quiet spot
and tune my banjo just so,
and scratch at the strings,
and plunk it,
and then bang it around some;
until we are acquainted again,
and have renewed our agreement
about something
I have never fully understood.

Then I pull aside the cover of my guitar bag.
Such a curious marriage
of wood and strings
and science and pain,
is this guitar.

And I am not yet awake
until I spend some time alone
with this curious instrument,
and hold it, and feel its weight
upon my shoulder,
and feel its strings and wood
beneath my fingers.

Then the fingers begin.
First they stretch,
then reach,
then crawl
and caress

the strings and the wood
as if feeling for something
that may have been left behind,
or for something that has always been there,
something, not even a good set of ears
might detect.

The fingers find a piece of that something,
they always do.
And the world begins to stir
from guitar slumber.
And the fingers and the strings and the wood
whisper sweet morning talk,
in a language known only
to strings and fingers and wood:
"Did you sleep well?"

The fingers remember
and the wood and the strings remember
and finally they murmur and giggle
and suddenly little guitar sounds
are about the room
where we tune again,
and welcome together
the many unknowns of this new day,
"Yes, I had a wonderful dream."

At last, the music smiles wakeful.
Yes, the fingers remember,
and the guitar thumps and hums

and rumbles and rings
as if it already knows
all the dreams ever dreamed,
by folks like me and you;
by folks like those strangers
in that room,
buzzing and chatting and waiting.

Chasing the Great Lead Belly

To get there, you must follow Interstate 20, going west out of Shreveport. It is a good highway and new. Then head north on Greenwood-Mooringsport Road on up through Longwood. Up there it won't seem much like Louisiana; or at least like the Louisiana a northern person might already have pictured in their mind.

As you drive, you'll see oil derricks scattered across the grassy fields. Their greasy, boney frames slowly bobbing, pulling crude from beneath the Louisiana soil. You'll pass through some patches of piney woods and if you listen, you'll hear birds singing in the trees. There'll be some sawmills around, and you'll see farms that grow mostly cotton, and corn that dries and yellows early compared to the corn crop in the north. Travel in the morning while it's still cool. You'll see the sunlight flicker through the webbing of the tall pine trees that line the road.

When you reach Blanchard-Latex Road, that's where you have to head back out west. And then you only have to go a mile or two before you come to Shiloh Baptist Church. It's on the south side of the road, and it's one of the nicest churches you'll see. It's big. And made out of yellow brick with a wide dirt driveway that swings all the way around to the side of the building. There is a locked barrier meant to keep cars and trucks from driving up to the building, but it's easy enough to step over if you want to leave your car parked along the road.

Further back, behind the church is the graveyard. It's quite a big graveyard, and it's fenced in, but the gate won't be locked. Straight down the center, almost all the way back, that's where Mr. Ledbetter rests; right beneath the big tree. It's as quiet as can be back there, and the bed of fallen pine needles and soft red earth will make it easy for you to walk without making much noise. He's got a big granite headstone that marks the spot, and if you look around some, you'll find that he sleeps in the company of a good number of his family. They say he was born near Mooringsport, which is a little farm town just north and west of Shiloh Church on the south side of Caddo Lake, not far from the Texas line. Some say he was born in 1889. Others say 1885. The headstone says 1889. His name was Huddie Ledbetter and he was the greatest American folksinger, song collector and folk song composer that ever lived.

Folks called him "Lead Belly," and of course, there's not too many still around that knew him when he was alive. And of those few who did know him, and were there to hear him sing and play, they are now getting up in years. There's not much written about him either. And when you read what little has been written about him, and hear what's been told of him, it gets pretty hard to decide exactly what is true and what's been made up. There's just not much left to go on, except what those who knew him can recollect. And the records.

If you listen to the records, the first thing you'll hear is his voice. It's not a pretty voice. It's rough and grainy and sounds as if some of the raw tones have been scraped right up out of his throat. And of course you'll hear his guitar; the driving, chomping munch of his big twelve string guitar.

It's sometimes difficult to understand what old Lead Belly is singing about on the records. He speaks and sings with the slurred and rhythmic inflection of one who was born and lived a long time in the deep south. And if you wanted to play along, you'd have to string your own guitar up with extra heavy gauge steel strings and tune them four or five notes low to imitate the sounds and voicings of the "boogie-woogie" piano. That's how Lead Belly played it. The records will tell you that.

After four or five listenings, you'll begin to measure the beautiful cadence of his language, and you'll find your foot tapping right along to the driving pulse of his guitar music. You'll begin to hear him, and you'll begin to understand some of the things that he is singing about.

After a dozen or twenty listenings, you'll begin to realize that the things he sings about are the very things you might sing about, had you half a mind to make up your own song or remake and fashion some old tune into a brand new piece - with your own words, about your own place, about your own feelings, about your own vision for a world that might someday be better than the one you're in right now.

After fifty, or a hundred listenings, his world and a whole culture of people will begin to unfold. You'll begin to imagine some of the places where Lead Belly lived and worked, and traveled - and played music.

He'll take you back to the prison camps and work farms where he spent almost a quarter of his life, toiling under the blistering Texas sun for twelve or fourteen hours a day, and coming back to camp in the evening to entertain the convicts until the late hours of night.

You'll begin to imagine the sounds and smells of Fannin Street, the red light district of Shreveport, where he first began to play music in the dance halls, saloons and whorehouses. Listen to Lead Belly. He sings as he talks and he talks as he sings.

And if you listen to him on the records, you might begin to get an idea of the tragic poverty and punishing circumstances under which southern black people had to live and work.

You'll hear him sing about New York City, where he moved with his wife Martha Promise, to record and find a new and politically progressive audience who loved and glorified him. He was a survivor, a tenacious competitor who was determined to become a success in the music business. But in those days, not only was it difficult for a black man to become a successful recording star, but especially so for a black man who played the blues, ballads and spirituals of the poor south whose topical material was adamantly critical of Jim Crow.

In New York, Lead Belly became friends with and would forever influence the music of Woody Guthrie, Brownie McGhee, Sonny Terry, Cisco Houston, a very young Pete Seeger, and countless others. You can hear them all making music together on the records.

He blazed a trail to Europe that black blues singers and musicians would follow for generations to come, singing for the foreign audiences who fell in love with his warmth, his characteristic intimacy and his stories and songs from the southern United States. But back home fame and commercial success somehow always escaped him.

After hundreds of listenings to the records, you'll find yourself wishing to talk to someone who actually heard and saw Lead Belly play. Someone who might be able to describe and show you exactly how to imitate the pounding, chattering and explosive guitar style that was Lead Belly's alone. And after hundreds of listenings you'll begin to see his music in the music of others. You'll find his weave of story, song and opinion in the delivery of others. And from then on, you'll start hearing him in every chorus of "Irene Goodnight;" and he'll be in the wail and moan of every lonesome, battered voice that you'll ever hear crying out the blues.

And somehow, he'll always be there whenever you see a group of children dance while singing,

You gotta jump down turn around to pick a bale of cotton,
you gotta jump down turn around to pick a bale a day...

Then you'll begin to realize how Lead Belly's own voice and music has traveled and spread right along with our own aural tradition to somehow transcend time, race, religion, culture and class. And you'll find yourself wanting to make up the kinds of songs that Lead Belly made up. Songs that for generations have been considered nothing more than old folk songs; songs that might at first appear dated, but are actually stubbornly timeless; songs that will forever breathe with life so long as humans gather to sing about their trouble, joy and hope.

And if you listened to the records that many times, you would soon find yourself wanting to get as close as you could to the place where Lead Belly's amazing journey through time began. And how many more times would you listen before you found yourself actually walking along through the paved and cobblestone streets of old Shreveport? Or driving the back roads of northwest Louisiana, looking and listening on the wind, believing you might catch a glimpse of the ghost you first heard on the records?

You wouldn't find him of course. All that is really left are the records. And all you could really do is stop and pay your respects.

The Awful Truth
About Your Life in the Arts

Some people come to the arts by design, some by accident. Either way, your life in the arts begins with a calling of one kind or another, and eventually leads to a point when you look around and realize you're in pretty deep, and a convenient way out is no longer available.

The practice of art is at first a practice of opening. There is much to be discovered and tested, and much to be experienced. Mistakes must be made, then paid for. With opening comes a filling up, and we often start by filling ourselves up with ourselves. But later, we begin to notice all sorts of other details. Our ears and eyes drink in rivers of minute motions and sounds and inflections. From time to time we find ourselves arrested by color and line, rhythm and narrative, overwhelmed by a swirling, unnamed context of shadow and light. When raw imitation finally gives way, we find ourselves glimpsing into something new and mysterious and special. It's a place to which we are naturally drawn and must learn to navigate without clear instructions.

Then comes the emptying. It is singing, it is dancing, and it is many quiet hours of private work. It is rehearsing and travel and more practice. It is strange places and sometimes strange people, and the food isn't always so good either. It is layers of heartache and worry, and over time the very core of your vulnerability gets revealed and laid bare.

And then we fill ourselves up again. With more images and sounds, but also with caffeine, alcohol, fried food and sometimes other things too. A kind of protection I guess. Then more people, more places, and the circle goes around and around, again and again.

You scan the horizon for the next new thing, and welcome back the familiar, all the while working to keep alive the youthful spark from which your course was first struck. Tonight will surrender to another dawn, Mother Earth will tilt again on her axis, leaving snowy winter in the place where autumn used to be. Cognition and metaphor dance within, coming and going like some ethereal tide. Old Man River, he just keeps rollin' along.

And now you're fifty. You don't have a retirement account to speak of, nor do you yet have that summer home by the lake. The odometer on the vehicle purchased just last year is already over a hundred thousand, and rent is due on the first. Your knee hurts and your back hurts; it's cold out, and gas is still over three-fifty a gallon. There are politics of all kinds to deal with, and your guitar needs new strings. It's life in the Arts, just as it's always been, just as it always will be.

And the awful truth about your life in the arts is that you are in the arts. You're not a rock star and you're not a celebrity judge on a TV show. You're not a politician nor are you CEO of a large corporation. You are not a spokesmodel for a shiny new product.

You also don't have a staff meeting this morning. That is, unless you decide to take the paper down to the cafe to sip coffee and think about what's coming up this week. Your sweatshirt and jeans will be fine.

And maybe when you get home, you'll have time to change strings and go over the new piece you've been working on. There are people you'll need to talk to this week, and there are people you'll want to avoid. There is writing to tend to, and travel plans to make.

There are appointments to keep, and that picture of you in the paper isn't so bad after all.

A few good hours working on your work is all it takes to remind you where you began, where this began. It feels good to hold your instrument again, to hear the sound of fresh strings ringing through the room and to feel again a familiar resonance within. Most people enjoy tinkering with these sorts of things while on vacation or in their free time. It's the thing you get to think about and work on, while the rest of the world is dealing with somebody else's problems.

Your life in the arts then, is about finding your own work to do and getting after it. Between periodic splashes of attention and money are longer stretches of grinding it out, week after week, month after month. It's a modest existence to be sure, and often the work is very humbling. Your day-to-day activities in the arts sometimes resemble those of a garbage collector or a waitress, or a busboy. You are mostly here to haul things around, serve others, and clean up again after you've finished.

To accept all of this is a choice each has to make. Learning to proceed with care and dignity takes time and effort, but the trail is marked and the way is well known. Bob Dylan, Van Gogh, Martha Graham, Steinbeck, Duke Ellington, Walt Whitman, Joni Mitchell, Beethoven and the rest, have all made this choice in one way or another, and come this same way before you. But you are not them. You're not any of them.

Still others follow behind; each looking and listening, making their way and making their art. Some are young and beautiful, moving like swans, singing like nightingales. Some are dark and distant and puzzling, with tattoos, facial hair, perhaps a porkpie hat, and clothing that is different than your own.

But you're not any of them, either. You can't ever be any of them. You can only be you. And that's the truth.

When a Tree Falls

We lost a tree during last Friday's storm. By the time I got home it was late and there it was, lying in the darkness, parallel to the south fence all wet and shiny and sad. It was an Ailanthus, otherwise known as the Tree of Heaven, and the rotting trunk snapped off in the wind about four feet from the ground, crushing the gate and the segment of the east fence that runs up to Bill's house out back. The tree destroyed the iron railing on Bill's back stoop, tore down the power and phone lines to his house, and the upper limbs dented the hood and cracked the windshield on the car parked next to the coach house. An Ailanthus packs a wallop.

Ailanthus is an odd kind of tree, and I don't remember seeing one before moving here. The trunk is tall and straight, and the smooth bark reminds me a little of an elephant's skin. The branches do not have a broad span and begin their reach what seems to be a long way up from the ground. When it was standing, my Ailanthus stood out like an oddball between the Scotch Pine and the White Spruce that shared its little plot, and the Ailanthus was nothing like my glorious ancient Sliver Maple, which shades most of the backyard. The fallen Ailanthus was twenty-five paces long, making it around a seventy-five footer. I feel kind of sorry for not learning its name, and not learning more about it before now. It's sort of like finding out after he died that your weird uncle Ed was an FBI agent. You wish you had known.

For the third morning in a row the men are here early with their chainsaw, ensuring that the folksinger remains sleep deprived, and discharging the unpleasant duty of reducing what's left of my Ailanthus into firewood and sawdust. It is 7:45, and already it is hot. The air is sticky and I can smell the smoke of one of the men's cigarettes. I hear them chatting and laughing between chainsaw bursts. Their chainsaw whines and screams and it makes me want to put a screwdriver through each of my ear drums.

A long time ago I worked for a tree company which was contracted to prune the trees in many of the cemeteries around the village where I then lived. Those on the crew with skill and experience were the only ones allowed to ride the cherry picker up to trim the top branches. The new guys on the crew did the other work. We maneuvered the dump truck which pulled the chipper, into a strategic position, collected the fallen limbs, and either fed them into the chipper, or if they were too big around, used a chainsaw to turn them into firewood and sawdust.

Before I was demoted to running the chipper full time; before I had backed it into a headstone with the name CANARY on it, I used two chainsaws to handle the limbs. Mostly I used a mid-grade saw, around two horsepower. For the trunks and bigger limbs though, I got to fire up the STHIL, with its long ominous blade and seven horse engine. That saw had a deep growl when it idled and an authoritative roar when it sliced through timber.

The men in the yard this morning, laughing and smoking and pushing their little saw past its limits could use that STHIL. This is their third morning here. With a seven horse STHIL, they would've been done on the first day in a few hours, tops. And they would have had enough time left over to beat the noon rush for an Italian beef at the Tasty Dawg.

Right around the time the men finish off the Ailanthus, the lawn mowers will begin. And then the power edgers and the blowers will follow. The garbage truck will be by later today and the garbage man will not like that pile of wood awaiting him. He will beep his horn again, and again the pieces of Ailanthus will resound with boom after boom as they tumble into the back of the garbage truck. The motorcycles, the delivery vans, service vehicles and moms in their minivans running errands or bustling off to appointments, will all barrel down my street, as will the guy down the block who heads off to work each afternoon in a rusting Chevy in need of a new exhaust system.

Now that it's summer, the world is noisy again. Muffled winter mornings, doors and windows sealed, are a distant memory, as soon will be my Ailanthus, my Tree of Heaven. "When a tree falls in the forest and no one is around to hear it, does it make a sound?" goes the philosophical riddle. Nobody in the neighborhood recalled hearing my Tree of Heaven crash to the ground, no one. Not Bill out back, not Kathy who lives above him, not Christine who lives in the big yellow house next door. Nor did the fellow who lives upstairs from her and works nights at the post office hear it. Believe it or not, the guy in the coach house whose windshield got smashed didn't hear it either. When a tree falls in the forest and no one is around to hear it, does it make a sound? The answer is yes. Listen for the chainsaw.

The Dying Miner

Greetings form Centralia, Illinois. Centralia is a town way down the center of our state, directly east of St. Louis, and not far from Salem, along Interstate 57. The director of the Centralia Museum is a jolly woman named Becky Ault. Becky used to be the mayor of Centralia and knows everything about her town. She reminded me I was now in the part of Illinois known as Little Egypt, and to tell the people up in Chicago that, "there is a place called southern Illinois in our state." And then she laughed.

About eighty folks attended the concert last night, held at the Centralia Museum, on the second floor of an old building on south Locust Street, which used to house the Kohl and Meyer Company. Most of those in attendance were older and are regular members of the museum. Hugh and Lovetta drove down from Bartonville for the show, and picking buddies Don and Frank came all the way over from Lawrenceville.

There is a great folk song with roots in Centralia, Illinois, based upon a tragic event which took place here in 1947. Woody Guthrie wrote it and called it "The Dying Miner." It is sometimes remembered as "Goodbye Centralia," and the folks here sure do remember it.

The Centralia Mine Disaster of 1947 is important in that a hundred and eleven men who went down beneath the Illinois prairie that morning to dig for coal, did not come back up when it was quitting time. The story made headlines across the country and led to important reforms in mine safety.

A rare opportunity was missed last night when I did not have "The Dying Miner" on my mind and ready to go for the folks at the

Centralia Museum. Before heading out this morning, I'll get over to the site where the Number 5 Mine Disaster took place and have a look around.

Wamac, Illinois

Wamac is only a couple miles south of Centralia, Illiniois and
is the town where the Number 5 Mine disaster took place in 1947.
I have come to Wamac to walk around and look around and get
a permanent picture in my mind of the place where the luck of
one hundred and eleven miners ran out and where bureaucratic
negligence received its due.

Wamac is a modest town, with modest homes and a modest
central business district. Just south of the main intersection is
the town park. A gravel road leads into the park past some new
playground equipment, a squeaking oil derrick and some small
buildings, which must get a lot of use in the summer months. Before
long, I found myself wandering the outfield of the Wamac ballpark,
which looked like it hadn't had a game played on it in several
seasons.

In the distance a woman walks past the playground, wearing blue
jeans and a white blouse. She strides through the grass with purpose,
toward the main road, clenching an immense handbag under her right
elbow. Beyond her to the south is the headquarters of an industrial
service company. Trucks are parked around the main building, as
are trailers bearing different kinds of heavy equipment, all ready
and waiting to solve one kind of a problem or another. The park is
bordered on the north by a mobile home settlement, and a road which
dead ends at a barricade.

It is late morning on a Tuesday. The air is clear and the
temperature mild, and southern Illinois is in mid-bloom. A plaque in
the park commemorates the Number 5 Mine Disaster of March 25,
1947. It lists the names of the men who lost their lives and gives a

brief account of the tragedy. Images of nameless men in their mining helmets are inscribed onto each side of the marble stone, and the nearby picnic shelter is named the "Mine No. 5 Shelter."

Not everyone knows that Illinois is coal country. Eighty-five of Illinois' one hundred and two counties have claimed coal mining as an industry. In coal's heyday one hundred and eighty-five mines operated throughout the state, employing over fifty thousand men. Not everyone also knows that Illinois is actually a collection of smaller states whose borders are mostly fuzzy.

In the north of course, is Chicago with its economic brawn, political muscle and international cosmos. Reaching west from Chicago are the river towns of Peoria, Rockford and the Quad cities, all early centers of industry, trade and commerce. In the middle of our state is the city-constellation that includes Springfield, Champaign-Urbana, Decatur, Bloomington-Normal and Danville, each cultivated from a fertile mixture of farming, academics, hard work, government and the railroads.

Farther to the south, Illinois actually spills into the Ozark region where the steep hills, bluffs and forests belie her reputation for flat black earth and cornfields. But in the part of Illinois that begins somewhere north of Carbondale and somewhere east of Belleville, coal mining is one of the things that still goes on. The work is still dangerous, and the divide between those who own the mines and those who do the mining is still distinct.

In March 1946, a little more than a year before the explosion took place in Mine Number 5, a committee of union officials appealed to then Governor Dwight Green, with a letter that has come to be known as the "Please Save Our Lives Letter."

"Governor Green this is a plea to you," the letter begins, "to please save our lives. Please make the Department of Mines and

Minerals enforce the laws at No. 5 mine...before we have a dust explosion like just happened in Kentucky and West Virginia."

Three of the four miners who signed their names to the letter were among those killed.

A man by the name of Driscoll O. Scanlan was a state mine inspector in those days. Scanlan campaigned tirelessly to get the Number 5 mine "rock dusted," a procedure that would settle and neutralize the volatility of the coal dust. Rock dusting is time consuming and expensive, and Scanlan's reports and letters went largely ignored. And in the end, his efforts to save the miner's lives proved futile.

In a town like Wamac, the day seems to unfold a little differently than it does in other places. There is a different pace and a different etiquette. The neighborhood streets are tree lined and quiet, and there are homes in need of repair. The churches show that these are people of faith, and the bars and roadhouses show that they know how to have a good time. In a town like Wamac it seems that the work gets done, the appointments are made, and the errands are run within the greater margins of struggle and poverty.

The sun will set tonight on the business district of Wamac, Illinois, and it will set on the neighborhoods, the trailer parks, the churches and the bars. Tonight the sun will set on the junkyard where a concrete slab covers the hole that was once the entrance to Mine Number 5.

I Can Be Bought, But I Can't Be Sold

While sipping black coffee this morning in the lobby of the Memphis Marriott, charging my laptop and charging my phone, it struck me that I may be different than many of you. I am certainly different than many of the conference people already milling around the atrium here at the Marriott, the site of the 2010 International Folk Music and Dance Alliance Conference.

We arrived late last night, loaded in, and met Kate and Bill from Duluth for a drink in the hotel bar. There we also met Dalis and Kim from Texas, James from California, Randall from somewhere in America, Stephen Lee from Madison and Sandy from Chicago, whose car had slid into a ditch on the drive down. Bunches of others I didn't recognize congregated at the bar, at the pool table and in the corners. Amid laughter, tired faces, hand shaking and hugging, the selling game was already begun.

Don't get me wrong Your Honor, I've not got a thing against selling. With my left hand on the Holy Bible, I swear to God that I truly understand how Life is Selling and Selling is Life. I further understand that the market in our particular end of the performing arts is depressed. Business is slow and the competition for work is stiff.

Of course I am glad to meet new people in my line of work. And of course, I'm particularly glad to meet those who may be interested in hiring me. But the whole practice of turbo-selling oneself and presenting oneself as a packaged, marketable brand and making a positive impact while comparing apps on one's iPhone seemed silly to me at midnight in a hotel bar at the end of a long travel day. I had been bouncing around the back box of a Vista-Crusier RV for the last twelve hours and was cranky and wrinkled and tired and cold. And I wanted to enjoy my overpriced glass of merlot without having to try to express my career plans for the next five-year term in the time span of a sound bite. There's my presentation for the evening. Thank you.

At a similar, but smaller conference some years ago, I was witness to a conversation revolving around the concept of the *elevator pitch*. An elevator pitch is a marketing tool. It is a prepared thing to have ready to say should you find yourself riding in an elevator with a person in your field who may be in the position to help you advance your career.

It goes like this. You're riding up to the seventeenth floor on the hotel elevator, headed back to your room with a six-pack of beer and a bag of Doritos, hoping the cable service includes the History Channel. The elevator stops at the fifth floor, and a fellow, prominent in your field, steps into the car, reads your name badge and says something like, "Oh you are so and so from Chicago. I've heard of you. What is it that you do?" A seasoned conference person is ever-ready to network and realizes he's got exactly twelve floors to make the exchange memorable. His elevator pitch is already cocked and loaded, and he fires away, hopefully hitting the target and dutifully impressing said prominent individual. Perhaps the exchange will result in something like a lunch date to further discuss an opportunity or project. Or perhaps it will simply lead to hooking up later for darts in the hotel bar at the end of the day. More likely the encounter will provide some common basis for an another association down the road. Whatever the benefit, it beats watching the History Channel with a bag of Doritos and a beer.

So having a tool like a good elevator pitch is a useful thing. Those who are also hip to the latest technology and trends in their field seem to always hold some kind of advantage. This stuff supplies material that strangers can jib jab about while they get to know one another. Whatever. Learning to handle oneself well in front of prospective buyers is essential in any trade and those who learn to do it well, do well. Selling is Life and Life is Selling.

I'm just not every time comfortable carrying on in a manner that is so continually on the make. When a guy asks me what inning it is in the ball game, I don't feel compelled to hand him a business card and my fee schedule. "Bottom of the sixth," I say. "Two on, two out, Konerko up."

I do have an elevator pitch, by the way, and it's a dandy. I didn't come up with it at a strategic peer-group session at a professional conference, nor was it conceived as the product of a consultation with a career coach. It came about over time by watching collected, poised people ease into situations that are both social and professional. I learned what my elevator pitch should not be by witnessing other aggressive types yammer away at their career goals and resume building. My pitch was further polished after observing still others doing their work in edgy anticipation. Yep, I've got a damn fine elevator pitch. And one of these years, I hope to corner Mr. Career Changer in a hotel elevator and lay it on him.

A long, long time ago, I had the privilege of meeting a man named Walter McGhee. Nobody called him Walter though. He was known the world over as Brownie. Brownie was a big man with an even bigger personality. He was a singer, guitarist and songwriter. For more than forty years he toured the globe with his partner Sonny Terry. Brownie was bright, articulate and talented. He was a hard thinker and a keen observer, a student of many things. Brownie was a one-of-a-kind.

Don't take it from me though, go look him up. Google him and search him out on iTunes. Find him singing and playing on YouTube. Give a listen to his Folkways stuff, and then go back and listen to his early recordings. Liner notes and internet web sites will tell you that Blind Boy Fuller was an early influence. But why not do something for yourself and go look up Blind Boy Fuller, and spend some time listening to him too? When you go back again to the early Brownie, see if you can detect the Fuller influence in Brownie's guitar phrasing, and in his singing. Go ahead and try. I'll bet you can.

Now find some of Brownie's last recordings - soulful, wise and beautiful. Brownie was into his seventies by then and had lost something in his guitar chops. You can hear that too, if you listen. But, something new and delightful emerges when some young instrumentalist gets to play fire behind the vocals of the great Brownie McGhee. You can hear it in the strings, and you can hear it in his singing. I'll bet you can.

So there I was on Brownie's patio a long, long time ago. He had just dished out his favorite ice cream to his guests and magically, about eight little children from the neighborhood appeared from nowhere at the precise time. "They know that Brownie dishes ice cream at two o'clock," he said smiling. Brownie had a beautiful smile.

We continued our visit over spoonfuls of butter-pecan. Brownie spoke while rolling a frosty glob around in his mouth. "Yes," he said, "I played a lot of dates over the years. By myself and with Sonny. You know," he continued, "I could always be bought, but I could never be sold."

During our brief visit, I remember Brownie often speaking in such philosophical riddles, and didn't always know exactly what he meant. Gradually I became less concerned that it might show ignorance if I asked him to clarify. It finally dawned on me that Brownie probably knew precisely how ignorant I was by watching me walk up the driveway.

"What does that mean?" I asked, "I can be bought, but I can't be sold?" He was smiling again and watching the little ones with melted ice cream running down their faces and arms. "It means that if someone likes what I do and wants to invite me to their place to play, then I will be glad to come. And we will work out the details and arrangement. It means that I am not going to stand on a street corner and wave a big sign that says, 'Hey everybody, come down here and hire Brownie McGhee.'" He laughed and said it again, "I can be bought, but I can't be sold."

The dog days are gone now,
a sad, sagging pooch
who one day wobbled
to his summer feet,
and hobbled off
tongue wagging swelter,
after lifting his nose to the wind,
and sniffing something
that smelled to him
like autumn.

Canada sends her regards;
a crystal cool answer
to prayers prayed by those
in the stuffy attic apartment
across the street.

Hello Canada,
the dog days were dry this year.
Me and the ancient maple out back
have been waiting.

July's blaze
parched her emerald span,
her broad leaves blistered
by insane August breath,
on the side where the sun
burned like a sky ember
each afternoon.

The sweet grass
beneath her cover, though,
and the picnic table too,
are still safe.
Well done.

From a Diner in Coffeyville

The piped in music here at the diner in Coffeyville is too loud, and it's bad. It's hard to think straight with this music playing, with this painful plate of chicken-fried steak in front of me. I thought it might be a safe bet to order chicken-fried steak in this part of the country.

The streets running east and west in downtown Coffeyville, Kansas are numbered, and the streets running north and south are named after trees. And along them stand a sad collection of sagging buildings and empty storefronts. The Midland Theatre is gone. Dirty glass and boarded up windows are everywhere, save for the diner, the pawn shop, the pool hall, the antique store, and a handful of other hangers-on who haven't yet heard that it's time to quit in Coffeyville.

The new Super Wal-Mart went up last year, just east of Coffeyville along the state route. You can't get there from downtown by walking, and a parking spot close to the front door is very hard to find.

You can buy nearly anything you want at the new Super Wal-Mart. You can get brown pants and car parts and groceries and liquor and new school clothes for the kids. You can get your eyes checked and your hair cut. You can join the Army.

"It's a ghost town," said Mr. Jay D. Foster, Coffeyville born in nineteen twenty-seven, about his hometown. "Eleven thousand souls still call Coffeyville home," he added, "and we are forty churches strong, including the Black Baptists east of the tracks."

There are bunches of banks too, in Coffeyville, and a very long time ago a gang led by the Dalton boys tried to rob two of them on the very same day.

Over on Eighth Street is the Dalton Raid Museum. Back when business boomed and the Coffeyville coffers flowed with cash and the streets buzzed with action, them Dalton boys and their buddies one night grew frisky. They hatched a plan that involved robbing two banks simultaneously. Not only would they get the money, but perhaps they would also be remembered for something not even the James gang could pull off.

At some point, this idea apparently seemed like a good one, for the morning of October 5, 1892 found the Dalton gang riding into town dressed in disguises and hell-bent on stealing enough money to set themselves up for the rest of their lives. Boys, they sure did mess up your clothes.

Word on the street spread quickly that the Daltons were back in town and looking for trouble. By the time the alarm sounded, the good citizens of Coffeyville were already armed with rifles and shotguns from the Isham Hardware on Union Street. They chased the boys back up the alley towards the place where their horses were tied, and in only a few minutes time, the whole thing was over.

Four defenders lay dead with just a single shot in them apiece, including the city marshall. Two fell right away in front of the First National Bank, and two others a little after, down the alley right near the jail. That's where you boys made your last run for it; where you got yourselves riddled with Winchester rounds and buckshot.

And then they laid you boys out on the sidewalk like four first prizes, right in front of the Condon Bank for all of Coffeyville to see. You were being made an example of then, that's for sure, and you are being made an example of now. Likenesses of your lifeless bodies are painted on the sidewalk at the very spot, recalling a photograph on display at the museum, taken after the failed raid. Nobody messes with the Condon Bank.

And now that the bones of downtown Coffeyville have been picked clean, I wonder about the buzzards who first smelled death and circled the sky over Coffeyville, Kansas. In came the chain restaurant boys, the chain motel boys, the chain auto parts boys, and the chain quick-mart boys. In came the Wal-Mart. They all applied for loans from the big money boys, and set up shop along the state route.

It's about the profit, just as it's always been, no matter who plans the holdup. And as I saw through the remainder of my chicken-fried steak, leather and sawdust and paste, I wonder about the towns where those vampires live, they who made the decisions to back the national chain businesses that bled downtown Coffeyville dry. I wonder where they buy their groceries and their hardware. I wonder where they get shoes for their kids. Do they get their hair cut in the same barber shop their fathers went to? Do they ask, "Say boy's, how's it goin' today?" when they walk in the door? In which diner do they order their eggs and coffee?

And I wonder what the citizens of Coffeyville thought they were defending the morning of the raid way back in 1892. Maybe the Daltons had tired of the work and worry. Maybe they were weary from being broke and hungry all the time. Perhaps the hangovers and loneliness became too much.

Maybe though, those boys saw something. And perhaps they saw it coming all along, even from way back then. And now, the downtown of Coffeyville, Kansas is just as dead as those Dalton boys are. And downtown Coffeyville will be less remembered. That's for sure.

God, I Used to Love That Game

March is here and the major league baseball teams have returned to training camp in Florida and Arizona. Across the country, boys like I used to be are right now in the weight room, and in the north, they trudge through the late winter snow, getting their running in, before the team meets up for pre-season practice. They coax friends into a game of catch in the cold, to work on their side arm relay, long toss or overhand curve. I can't help but be swept up a little with this ritual, and every year around this time I think again about heading down to the batting cage across town with a roll of quarters, just to see. Probably takes dollar bills now.

This time of year is special in ways that are sometimes hard to explain. Maybe it's simple nostalgia, but perhaps it is something else again. The return of spring - the return of baseball - marks the rebirth of the year, a renewal of the spirit and the resurrection of hope that the new season may be fruitful.

My grandfather was a professional baseball player. Some years ago, we found his contract among a stash of his earthly possessions and documents, in the back of one of the closets at home. He was a pitcher and outfielder and as best as I can remember, he played for a club in the low minor leagues somewhere out in Nebraska. I once did a little research and concluded his team was an affiliate of what is now the Baltimore Orioles in the American League. According to family lore he had to leave the club sometime during his first season to help out with some matter at home.

My dad was a baseball player too. He was tall and lanky and played first base for a semi-pro team on the west side of Chicago, and he could really hit. After he married mom and started a family, he played sixteen inch softball each summer in local leagues around Cicero, Illinois, including a couple seasons with a Windy City team in Chicago. As soon as his firstborn son expressed an interest in the game, down to the store we all went. My oldest brother came home with a fine new Rawlings glove. The rest of us got gloves too, and we began. Dad's family responsibilities had transformed his game into pitching underhanded to his little kids, teaching them how to keep their back foot still, hands back and eye on the ball.

I wouldn't say that baseball was like a religion in our family, but it was always there, and something we always seemed to return to. We cheered for both the White Sox and the Cubs, and had our favorite players of course, but it was the game we really liked. When our family moved west to an unincorporated area near LaGrange, Illinois, our new backyard was three-quarters of an acre, complete with a backstop and a row of hedges which designated the outfield wall. Center was short, left was deep, and a big sycamore tree shaded right. Periodically we custom-mowed the grass to indicate the foul lines and infield dirt.

By the time I learned to love Jesus in Sunday school, I had already loved baseball that much. And I still do love baseball that much, but I can no longer play, so it's a little different now. My legitimate career in the game ended a long time ago, a mere glimpse of possibility and hope.

I mostly played center field and was fast and smart. I had a good arm and was a young fly chaser with excellent range. At the plate I had a good eye and could hit for average, with only occasional power. I could draw a walk, beat out a bunt, steal a base, drive in a run or move a runner along. No "I" in team.

Just about every ballplayer who hangs around the game long enough earns himself a nickname, even in Little League. Someone whose name begins with an "Mc" almost always becomes "Mac" or "Mick" for the rest of his baseball life. One season we had two kids on the team, each with red hair and freckles. They were "Big Red" and "Little Red," respectively. Boys called Robert or Edward by a teacher in class are automatically "Bobby" and "Eddie" on the diamond. Last names are often shortened so they can be blurted out quickly. A young fellow on our team with the last name Burson, became "Burse," or "Bursey," depending. Other nicknames emerged based upon one's personality. I'm thinking now of a fellow who pitched for another team in the Babe Ruth League in the late 1970s with the nickname "Weed."

I wasn't a smoker of anything during my baseball days. Didn't drink neither. Didn't chew and was still a little shy around the girls. I was also usually quiet around the boys while they jocked around before and after the game. I was a clean kid, and my practice habits and demeanor earned me the nickname, "Preacher." On good days I remember hearing, "Way to go Preacher," and "Nice catch, Preacher," and "Bring him in, Preach." I was naturally thrilled, like the others, the one summer a small bunch of us got scouted, but my baseball dream lingered for only a short time thereafter. I played one more season in Babe Ruth and rode the bench for a portion of another in semi-pro, and then it was all over. Around that time I was starting to learn to play the banjo.

Over the years, my travels as a musician have brought me to many small towns and rural communities. And in springtime, one senses the return of baseball with the smell of clean country air and the sight of a newly plowed farm field. While on the road, it was once my habit to seek out a ball game during down time. I have attended minor league games played by the Fort Wayne Wizards, the Quad City Angels, the Burlington Bees, the South Bend Hawks, the Toledo Mud Hens, the Madison Mallards and a few others. I have also been witness to college and high school games and the experience has always been the same.

Pekin, Illinois is just down river from Peoria in the heart of some very serious baseball country. Once while in Pekin with the afternoon off, I got to sit in the stands munching popcorn with my book as the Pekin Dragons varsity team held an afternoon workout. I was keeping a kind of travel journal in those days, and the entry from that day went like this:

April, 18, 2002

...Pekin might be the place where summer always lives. It's been warm in Chicago for this time of year, but when I arrived in Pekin, summer was already here. The mornings have been sunny and warm and clear, and all evidence suggests it has been this way for some time now. By afternoon the breeze picks up each day and puffy mountains of clouds fluff way up in a high summer sky...

Many of the children I have visited this trip have knees and elbows and chins already scraped and bandaged or scabbed. One boy had a shiner behind his Scotch-taped-together glasses, and one little girl had a blue fiberglass cast on her broken arm. The boys at the high school held ball practice at Dragon Field on Wednesday afternoon, their lean torsos glistening shirtless in the afternoon sun. I ate a bag of popcorn and from the grandstand watched them go through their drills, and listened to them shout and laugh and work hard at their play.

Maybe Pekin is the place where the sky is always friendly and high, where the wind always blows warm from the southwest, and where the lazy river is always churning green and brown. Maybe it's

always two months till school is out in Pekin, Illinois, and maybe
it's the place where the farm fields are always newly planted, so
there isn't so much work to do until the corn and soy beans need
cultivating. Maybe Pekin is the place where the boys get to play
baseball all the time.

God, I used to love that game.

Talcott, West Virginia

A hundred miles south of Charleston, West Virginia, a sleepy town called Talcott lies nestled on the banks of the beautiful Greenbriar River. Beckley and Hinton are the nearest big towns if you're looking on a map. While traveling last summer, I stopped in Talcott because it is where the famous contest between John Henry and the steam drill took place, and is where one of the great American ballads was born.

There are many facets to the legend of John Henry, but there is no longer any written proof that the contest ever took place, or that a man named John Henry even existed. All the records of the C & O Railroad were lost in a fire in the 1870s.

It is mid-August and after several dry years in a row, many a Midwestern lawn and valley has been reduced to hardscrabble. But West Virginia is still lush and green this late summer. The John Denver song plays through my mind, as it always does when I drive through this part of the country, "Almost heaven..."

A sign along the interstate promises a Welcome Center and I pull in. The little gal behind the counter giggled a bit when I asked if she had any brochures about Talcott and John Henry. She said, "Oh sure, let me get you one." But it turned out she was out of them. In Lewisburg, all the brochures were gone from the Chamber of Commerce but the gal thought there might be some down at this restaurant or that. Gone. Gone. I'm thinking now that I'm not the only one chasing the John Henry legend this summer.

Brochure or not, I climb back into the truck and head for Talcott. It's quiet out on these back roads, and Route 12 is especially pretty as it follows along the Greenbriar. If there ever was a contest to determine which rivers were properly named, the Greenbriar would surely be a finalist. It is green and lazy, with tall rocky sides, and since the dawn of creation it has been cutting its way through the sweeping beauty of these Southern mountains. With the sun having crested past midday, the light on the hillsides has turned the treetops into a fluffed blanket of warm greens and yellows.

Pretty soon I'm on the edge of a town and there's a sign out in front of the graveyard that reads, "Talcott, West Virginia, Home of the John Henry Legend." The main road in Talcott parallels the railroad tracks, the Chesapeake and Ohio, the same line John Henry and his crew worked for. On this side of the tracks is a gas station, a soda fountain, a hardware and a restaurant. Some modest homes are squeezed in along the main road before the cross streets sweep upward and disappear again into higher ground.

On the other side of the tracks are what look to be some still modest, but nicer homes. Looks like an old hotel that is something else now and a compact church, its steeple rising above anything else around. A backdrop of green curtains the entire town, for we are in the West Virginia highlands and Talcott is low, near the river. Before I knew it, I had blown through town and had to turn around in the parking lot of an abandoned roadhouse on the west end. I drove back and parked in front of the soda fountain.

It's a tiny place decked out in 1950s sock-hop decor. I asked the fellow, a real nice man, about the John Henry legend. He says, "We're out of brochures. Let me run next door to the hardware, I'm sure she's got one there."

He's got an old red Coca-Cola dispenser. I lay a dollar on the counter, pull a bottle out and flip off the cap. I'm looking at all the stuff on the shelves and the pictures on the wall. There's Elvis and James Dean and Marilyn Monroe. There's a half-dozen model trucks.

And there on the back wall is a collection of John Henry statues. All small, some dramatic and some kind of comical.

The guy comes back huffing and puffing. "This is the last one she had." I thank him, and he gets me thirty-five cents change. We chat about the legend and the festival they have each autumn, John Henry Days. I ask him if the contest took place anywhere near here, thinking it must have happened out in the sticks somewhere. Reminding me we were already in the sticks, he points out the window and says, "Drive up that gravel road and follow the tracks. It's a quarter mile down. You'll see both tunnels."

And there are two tunnels running through Big Bend Mountain in Talcott, West Virginia. There's the new one built in 1972 called Big Bend Tunnel, that is still in use. Next to it, perhaps thirty yards to the right, tucked in the shade, is the Great Bend Tunnel. That's the one where they say John Henry whipped the steam drill and according to some accounts, died from a burst blood vessel in his brain - an aneurysm.

It's dark and dank and real muddy in the Great Bend Tunnel, as if it rains all the time. In the 1870s it took more than a thousand men two years to blast and dig their way clean through. More than two hundred of them died along the way. Mostly from cave-ins, but many from sickness and from injuries sustained while fighting.

The tunnel is more than a mile long and if you walk way to the right edge of the opening and scan the darkness you can see a pinhole of light at the other end. More than likely there have been cave-ins since the tunnel was abandoned, and I wouldn't be surprised to learn there were piles of junk dumped in there or some old cars. But you can see the pinhole if you look for it.

There's empty pop bottles and empty beer bottles and cigarette butts all over the place and spray paint graffiti on the mossy walls.

There's garbage and evidence that this is a place people travel to see and a place where locals hang out and leave their mark.

I wondered some more about John Henry. I sat on a rock and unfolded the brochure. No one knows where or when John Henry was born it says. It says he was a former slave, and was renown as a singer and a fine banjo player. It says he planed down the handles of his sledge hammers thin to maximize the speed of his swing. It says the stories about him were passed down from those who worked with him and those who were there the historic afternoon when he beat the steam drill. Many believe he used two shortened hammers, one in each hand, and wore out two sets of shakers during the contest.

It says there is evidence that John Henry's wife is buried in the graveyard on the edge of town. Some say that John Henry didn't die after the great contest, that he lived almost to completion of the tunnel and was then felled by a great cave in. They reason then, that John himself may be buried in that same graveyard.

I folded up the brochure and walked one more time to the great opening that is Great Bend Tunnel, where somewhere down in the darkness two hundred men died a long time ago. And somewhere in that darkness the sounds of men working and the sounds of sledge striking steel echoed through the valley here in Talcott, West Virginia. From somewhere in that same darkness one of those men grew to become a folk hero of worldwide fame, a universal symbol of strength and spirit who millions now know as John Henry, the Steel Drivin' Man.

On the way back to the main road, I stopped and picked up a couple of railroad spikes for souvenirs. Just past the abandoned roadhouse where I turned around earlier in the afternoon, the road pitches up a steep grade and winds to the top of Big Bend Mountain. There's a small lookout park on the top called John Henry Park.

You can see the new railroad tracks and the old railroad bed down below. In the 1970s an iron statue of a huge African holding a sledge hammer was erected and dedicated to the memory of John Henry one hundred years after completion of the Great Bend Tunnel.

The dedication ends with a prayer, "May God grant that we always respect the great and strong and be of service to others."

Bowling for Christmas

The chances of a pro bowler rolling a perfect game are around one in five hundred, roughly the same percentage of babies born with a condition called hydrocephalus.

Hydrocephalus is more common than Down syndrome or deafness, and a baby born with it has a body that can't properly circulate fluid within their little brain. In pronounced cases the cerebrospinal fluid builds up and begins to stretch the still soft bone tissue of their skull, enlarging the size of their head. As the child grows, the amassed fluid will slowly begin to put pressure on the brain itself, and that can cause all sorts of problems.

It's spring-chilly today and the sky is hazy. And it feels a little strange to be googling the term 'hydrocephalus' while killing time between shows at the MainStreet Theatre here in Michigan City, Indiana. I'm sitting in a lovely coffee shop just a short walk from downtown, and right across the street from Lighthouse Place Outlet Mall, a huge outdoor shopping extravaganza.

After a busy winter, signs of fatigue are again knocking at the door. My voice is a little scratchier, my bones a little achier, and I might admit to being a little grumpier too. Out the window, traffic and shoppers lumber towards the mall. The giant cooling tower from the Michigan City Power Plant lurks in the background, spewing a column of steam into the March sky. As I type and sip and look things up on the internet, a touch of melancholy has settled in with the afternoon.

Early in my performing life, the Lighthouse Place hired me to stroll the grounds with my banjo and guitar. As I remember, the mall was pretty new then too, and a season-long army of entertainers was engaged to help create a festive hubbub for the shoppers and mall walkers. Was it twenty years ago? Probably more. I think it was autumn. I seem to remember crisp air and leaves and bits of trash swirling along the concrete walkway. I also seem to remember there were not so many people to play for.

In those days, much like in these days, I was willing to accept just about any booking that came in. Between coffeehouses and bar gigs, summer festivals and an occasional concert, I was able to cobble together a modest living by playing at places like Lighthouse Place. There were also the Cub Scout troops, the women's clubs, the street fairs, the nursing homes and assisted living residences. I sat with children in daycare centers and at birthday parties. I entertained at family barbecues and at church picnics.

Over the years, the list of more unconventional venues I ventured into, grew to include a plentitude of elementary schools, and an equal number of libraries all over the place. For six years I helped bring music to a string of homeless shelters across Chicago and made regular visits to the Rehabilitation Institute, the Marklund Home for Children, the psychiatric ward at St. Joseph's Hospital, Hines Veterans Hospital and other institutions for the handicapped, the addicted, the sick and the needy.

I promise you, the ability to play a banjo and guitar, even marginally well, will result in many adventures, and more than a few curious circumstances. But what the heck, I was out of the warehouse and out on the road playing music, teaching a little and learning a lot, no longer lifting boxes all night long to make a living. I remember counting up the money at the end of one of those early years, astonished that my income from music and teaching had surpassed what I made from earlier, less attractive forms of employment.

Awash in memories from what today feels like a twenty-year mad dash through a jumbled maze of faces and shadows, bright light and long, all-night car rides, the image of a kaleidoscope comes to mind. Bits of broken glass, cobalt blue, amber and deep forest green, tumble and shimmer in a long tube of mirrors.

Before today, I did not know the word hydrocephalus. I wound up searching it out on the internet this afternoon because of a woman I once met who had it, a woman that I have never forgotten. I don't remember her name, but she lived at the Glen Oaks Nursing Home in Northbrook, Illinois. She was a little person, a dwarf, whose body was small, whose head was large and whose very sweet eyes were the color of robin's eggs. I met her on Christmas Eve, the same year of my first visit here to Michigan City, to strum and sing while strolling the walkways of Lighthouse Place.

This afternoon, only pieces from that year fall to memory. It was the middle of December, and a woman's voice, husky and urgent, is on the phone. She asks if I am who I am and I said that I was. She said who she was and continued, "I'm the activity director at Glen Oaks Nursing Home in Northbrook. It's really more like Skokie," she said, "but we're in Northbrook." Something about that last part made her laugh, which triggered a craggy smoker's cough.

She was hoping I might be able to help her out. She had planned a Christmas party for the residents on her floor, and the entertainer she had scheduled had just cancelled. "I know it's like the last minute," she said, "but I was hoping you might be available." She laughed again and then coughed. "I can pay you fifty dollars."

I paged through my appointment book knowing that a flurry of holiday bookings had already been arranged. Between those and what remained of my teaching schedule for the year, the rest of December was pretty filled up. Fifty dollars was an okay offer, but not terribly exciting. I sometimes got as much as seventy-five for a similar type of job, and one time got a hundred.

Also, these last minute jobs can turn out to be difficult. Perhaps someone really had just cancelled, but then again the line about a cancellation is sometimes a cover for a lack of planning. It could be a sign of a disorganized organization, and I had already experienced my share of those. Details get lost or forgotten, dates and times mysteriously change, or a promised check never arrives.

"I'm looking pretty booked up for the rest on the month," I say, "What's the date of your party?"

After a moment she said, "Christmas Eve."

I looked up December 24 in my book, a little relieved to find I already had something scheduled for that afternoon.

"I'm so sorry," I said to her, "I'm already scheduled for the afternoon of the twenty-fourth."

"You're busy in the afternoon?" she said.

"Yes," I said, "I'm sorry I won't be able to help you out this time."

Another pause. "Our party is in the evening," she said. "I was hoping you could come around seven."

"On Christmas Eve?"

"I know you might already have something going on," she said, "but my volunteers and I have planned a Christmas celebration for the residents, and we were hoping for some special entertainment before they open presents. You know, they really, really love music."

I had been looking forward to Christmas Eve with my parents and brothers, and to a good rest through the holidays. It had already been a busy year and things were looking up. I had just started teaching at the Old Town School of Folk Music in Chicago, and for the first time it began to feel like I might do okay at all of this. I'd always been pretty good at worming out of things I didn't want to do, and whether I turned her down now or not wasn't the question. While flipping through my internal rolodex of excuses, her voice broke the bit of silence.

"Look," she said, "these are special needs people and they have so little. We're putting this together out of our own pockets and on our own time. We're just trying to give them something for the holidays."

She had me. Anything else said at this point would only have come across sounding like, "Bah, humbug." I would have to break the news to my mom that I had a job on Christmas Eve.

"I'll give you sixty," she said, and she coughed.

Eight days later, I pulled up to the front entrance of the Glen Oaks Nursing Home in Northbrook, Illinois. It was cold and dark and it was Christmas Eve. I unloaded my gear while visions of roast beef with potatoes and gravy, and glasses of rum-laced egg nog danced through my head.

Glen Oaks was once a swank hotel, but at some point was converted to a nursing facility. I remember very few holiday decorations in the lobby. And there weren't any families or staff people around, save for the receptionist behind the counter. Running a little late, I headed towards the elevator, guitar and banjo in tow. Up I went.

The elevator doors opened and the little woman with hydrocephalus, the gal with the sweet eyes was there to greet me.

"Oh welcome," she said. She backed away a little shy, as I

stepped off the elevator. Her voice was light and cheerful, "We're so glad you could make it to our party tonight."

I set down my instruments and bag and Laura, the husky-voiced woman on the phone, rushed over to introduce herself. "Thank you so much for coming," she said extending both hands, "and Merry Christmas." She looked directly into my eyes and the sincerity of her greeting was striking. "Yes, Merry Christmas," the little gal chimed in from somewhere behind Laura, nodding and smiling.

Laura introduced me around to several of her volunteers and a handful of the special needs residents already gathered in the common area of their floor. A slender Christmas tree stood in the corner with a pretty plastic angel on top. There were lights and homemade ornaments and a life-sized cardboard image of a rosy-cheeked Santa Claus enjoying a bottle of Coca-Cola, was taped to a nearby wall. I remember being nervous and feeling unsettled about the whole assignment.

I headed back down to the truck to haul up the sound system, wondering what in my prior life could have possibly prepared me for the experience about to take place. Growing up in school, there had almost always been a special needs kid or two, but until that evening at Glen Oaks, I of God-given health and well being had never been so in the minority of so many other adults so physically and mentally disadvantaged.

My recollection of the evening from there is vague. I remember how curious all the folks were as I set up my gear and plugged things in. There was an older gent who walked all bent over, smiling all the time and mouthing words I couldn't understand. There were younger people confined to state-of-the-art wheelchairs who weren't able to do much more than receive stimuli and wiggle with glee or moan for attention. There was a woman born without eyes who smiled quietly. Still others sat along the wall, with a fixed gaze or rocking in their seat, focused on a memory or a vision that no apprentice folksinger could ever be privy to.

Finally it was time to begin. Laura and the volunteers got everybody situated, seating themselves among the bouncing, rocking, squealing and silent group of perhaps thirty residents. The volunteers wiped mouths and noses, held hands, clapped rhythm and searched into vacant eyes talking and singing, hoping to coax a trace of a smile.

We sang "Jingle Bells" and "You Are My Sunshine." Someone then asked for "Jingle Bells," and so we sang it again. I played some other folk songs too, perhaps "When the Saints Go Marching In," and "This Land Is Your Land." I remember aiming for the familiar while feeling my way through the program.

The rhythm of guitar music became exciting in ways I had not considered before that night. I remember at one point looking at the cardboard Santa and then to the angel at the top of the tree, hoping the music might somehow transcend this peculiar chasm, and in some way unite the array of destinies gathered within the room.

There was silence, then a gasp and a squeal when I opened the case to reveal a five-string banjo. Whatever inherent happiness may reside in the sound of a five-string banjo, rest assured friends, that from that night forward, one more thankful than I for such magic, has never walked the earth. I don't remember what I played, but I remember it wasn't too fast. I remember the strings ringing and sound darting across the room like little rays of light, then dissolving like stardust from Tinkerbell's wand above the heads of those lovely listeners.

One of the volunteers began clapping rhythm and a kind of honest festivity flared up and made itself known. Another volunteer mimicked a square dance with a slow-footed gent, another held both hands of a wheelchair-bound lass and each of them beamed. Laura kept an eye on me, nodding assurance as I navigated through the program, and I noticed again the little gal with the robin's eggs eyes. She was smiling, looking right at me. And she seemed happy for all of us, every one.

I remember our wobbling, beautiful voices on "Silent Night," so slow and solemn, and the pure merriment in "We Wish You a Merry Christmas," a song I had never admired until I heard The Weavers sing it on a scratchy old lp.

Laura came rushing over and whispered, "Do you know 'Santa Claus is Coming to Town'?" I nodded and as she turned, I called out, "Hey everybody, Santa Claus is coming!" and the room erupted. I had done bunches of similar Christmas programs before, and assumed Laura had arranged for Carl the Janitor or somebody, to don the red suit and beard and stuff a pillow under his blouse and make an appearance. At Glen Oaks though, on that Christmas Eve, Carl had already gone home for the night. No suit, no beard, no pillow. Laura turned back and announced to everyone, "Santa is busy tonight but he stopped by earlier today." The room erupted again.

I began the happy verses and at once all attention turned to Laura and the volunteer who schlepped in a huge box wrapped in Christmas paper. Those who could, ganged around them like ball players on the winning side after the last out of the world series. Those who couldn't wiggled in their chairs, smiling wide and bouncing.

The package was placed next to the tree and someone handed me a paper cup of Kool-Aid and a napkin of cookies. Laura quieted the group and I began wrapping wires and putting instruments away. Two volunteers kneeled and dramatically opened the package. The group huddled in close.

"Look," said the volunteer, "it's a bowling set!" Silence. She opened the box and out came ten plastic pins, a black plastic bowling ball and a plastic floor mat indicating where the pins ought to be set up. The volunteer held up a pin with one hand and the black ball with the other. She stood the single pin on end and demonstrated how a rolling ball could make it tumble to the floor.

"Oh, it's a bowling set!" said the little gal, "It's a bowling set!" She leaped with excitement and her glee began to spread. "Let's set it up," someone said. "Let's play bowling," said someone else. "Yes, let's play bowling," became the chorus.

Everyone looked towards Laura and Laura looked at her watch. It was already past eight-thirty and Laura looked tired. Finally she spoke. She thanked the volunteers by name, and looked at her watch again and said, "I don't think we're going to have time to play bowling tonight. I'm so sorry, but it's getting late. We have to get home to our families."

Laura and her volunteers still had to clean up and get everybody off to bed. There were pajamas to be changed into, bathrooms to visit, teeth to brush, medications to administer, wheelchairs to deal with and what all else before the people on this most special floor of the Glen Oaks Nursing Home were all nestled snug in their beds.

"Tomorrow is Christmas," said Laura. "We'll set up the bowling game tomorrow." Her words hung in the air.

Before today, I did not know the word hydrocephalus. I wound up searching it out on the internet this afternoon at the coffee shop, because of a woman I once met who had it and who I have never forgotten. She was a little person, a dwarf, whose body was small, whose head was large and whose very sweet eyes were the color of robin's eggs.

And her voice was light and cheerful when she exclaimed, "We'll have bowling for Christmas!" And after a pause came the words I want to always remember.

She said, "We have so much to be thankful for."

Another Thought

I have always liked words. I have always liked the way words made me feel while reading, and how an entire world of thought never before considered, can be brought forth from some simple words on a page.

I have always liked the sounds of words. I have often wondered how spoken expressions are spontaneously put together by our minds, and our mouths. They are a kind of music, and I have always enjoyed listening to others' voices, imagining the places within from which they are speaking. I like the way some words feel in my mouth when I am speaking, and I sometimes like to read out loud, just to hear the sounds of the words.

For a long time now, I have been a scribbler of words. I have never been properly motivated nor prepared, to keep an organized journal for any length of time. As a result, the greatest portion of my writing has evolved from an abiding impulse to scribble.

I have scribbled down descriptions of different scenes and experiences, and have dashed off many hasty observations on politics, books, movies, music, teaching and other subjects. Every once in a while some small piece of writing will emerge that requires me to stay a little longer, to pay closer attention, and to consider the language one more time.

My wayward process of scribbling and editing, rereading and listening, has over the years then, yielded this humble collection.

Over time, I have shared some of these drafts with others in various circumstances. Some of the pieces have already appeared in one form or another, and some are brand new. For this collection, each has been revisited and polished anew.

I am grateful for the help and seasoned guidance of Lisa M. Lilly, author of two novels, *The Awakening,* and *The Tower Formerly Known as Sears*. Lisa is also an attorney, and I've known her since she was a little girl. Her older brother Tim was one of my early guitar buddies, and her parents Frank and Helen, and other brother Keith, were like family in those days. In the essay *North Platte, Nebraska,* I remember Tim and our motorcycle adventure together.

And I am thankful for Marianne Mohrhusen and her quiet patience. She's a good listener with a keen sense for proper grammar.

Enjoy.

MD
autumn, 2013
Riverside, Illinois

MARK DVORAK is a musician, teacher and songwriter. When not on the road, he lives along the DesPlaines River in Riverside, Illinois and teaches at Chicago's Old Town School of Folk Music.

He has given concerts in almost all of the United States and has made visits to Finland, Canada and Ireland. To date, Dvorak has released sixteen albums of traditional and original music, including Waterbug's acclaimed *Time Ain't Got Nothin' On Me*.

Dvorak has won awards for children's music, journalism and was honored in 2008 with the Woodstock Folk Festival Lifetime Achievement Award. In 2013, he received the FARM Lantern Bearer Award from Folk Alliance International.

The Chicago Tribune has called him, "masterful," and the Fox Valley Folk Festival describes him as "a living archive of song and style." In 2012, WFMT Midnight Special host Rich Warren named Dvorak, "Chicago's official troubadour."

Mark Dvorak is available for concerts, readings and workshops. For more information, visit him on the web at www.markdvorak.com.